RON'S WAR

To JOHN

With best wishes &
kind regards

Ron

Ron WARBURTON

RON'S WAR

The Personal Chronicle of a Flight
Engineer of a Lancaster in Wartime

Ron Warburton

RW Press

Copyright © 2010 Ronald W. Warburton

All rights reserved. No part of this book may be reproduced or transmitted in any form or by any means without written permission of the author.

ISBN: 978-0-9831788-0-4

RW Press
8 Sunnydown Court
Hendon Avenue
Littlehampton,
West Sussex, U.K.

150 Eustis Avenue
Newport, RI 02840
U.S.A

Dedication

This book is dedicated to all my fellow Flight Engineers, who are rarely mentioned, and only occasionally in passing in historical war books, and for example, barely appeared in the film of the Dam Busters, or any other film I have seen.

Acknowledgements

The writing and accuracy of this story was immeasurably helped by Margaret Warburton, my wife of 62 years, who investigated and found that The National Records Office at Kew has the original records of the missions, activities, and history of all squadrons of the R.A.F. These Operational Record Book entries were based on the interrogation of crews immediately on their return from operations.

Margaret's patience and help in finding and printing the relevant sheets of 218 Squadron's activities was of inestimable help to me in my task. Left to my memory it would have been a very different picture, as at 84 years of age my memory is definitely suspect. Also, her constructive comments in the first reading and editing of this story were of inestimable help.

Thank you, Margaret.

I also wish to express my gratitude to my son Roger, who did a fantastic job of editing and laying out the book, and in providing such constructive remarks.

Thank you, Roger.

I am also indebted to Alf Cowley, the Australian pilot who flew the aircraft, finished my education and recorded detailed information in his log book of all training and operational flights.

When I spoke to him of my project, he photocopied his log-book and sent it to me. He was a brilliant pilot, attested to by his ratings and assessments throughout his career in the R.A.A.F.

Thank you, Alf.

I would also like to mention Marjorie Griffiths, one of the W.A.A.F. drivers who formed the 218 Squadron Association and is still keeping it going today. A room in her garden is full of photographs of all those who flew and serviced the aircraft, and all who contributed to running the Squadron.

A special note of my gratitude goes to the ground staff, the unsung heroes who serviced and repaired the aircraft we flew. Their skill, conscientiousness and diligence made the aircraft so reliable and dependable for us to fly.

A word of thanks should also be made to the background staff that did the administration, cooking and all the household tasks that were necessary to keep a squadron airborne.

I should also thank my crew, Alf the pilot, Charlie the navigator, Bob the bomb aimer, Pete the rear gunner, Norman the mid-upper gunner, and Mack the wireless operator. In my view, this was the best crew of the best Squadron in Bomber Command, an opinion borne out by the all the assessments made of us. Without the team work and cooperation of all we would not have survived the war.

Now just names in the history of the R.A.F, it should be mentioned that we survived but 55,000 aircrew did not.

I'd like to thank the staff at the Image Sales and Licensing Department at The Imperial War Museum for their help in obtaining copies of their Photographs, and expediting the permission process.

I'd also like to thank Hugh Alexander, the Image Library Deputy Manager at The National Archives, at Kew, Richmond for helping with permission to use the copies of the Operations Record Book.

I'd like to thank Danny Howell, Sales Executive at the Daily Mail for permission to publish Alf's copies of the stories from the Daily Mail and the Daily Sketch.

We all owe a debt of gratitude to those professionals who maintain the records. Their patience in guiding me through the legal details is much appreciated.

Littlehampton, 2010

"The fighters are our salvation but the bombers alone provide the means of victory."

--Winston Churchill, to the War Cabinet,
3rd September, 1940.

CHAPTER 1

EARLY DAYS

I was born in 26 Taff Embankment, Cardiff, a road along the west bank of the river Taff almost opposite the Cardiff Arms Park, now the Millennium Stadium. It is said that when it was built, the changing rooms were put under the North Stand so that the singing of the Welsh Crowd would intimidate the opposition and inspire the Welsh team. For those who have not experienced this, the Welsh are a nation of singers and will burst into song at every opportunity, mostly hymns, but the harmony of voices has to be heard to be believed.

My memories of my early days make me realize that I was a lonely boy, although I did not recognize it. My first recollections are of living in St. Thomas Street, Swansea, a short steep hill overlooking Swansea docks. At the bottom of the hill was the main road to Port Tennant with a large high fence boundary to the Docks. Between the fence and the docks were railway lines, which were used when coal was brought down from the Merthyr Valley to the ships.

I attended St. Thomas Elementary School, which was on a hill overlooking the River Tawe, about a mile from my home. The only memories of school life are of bowling in the cricket nets in the school playground on concrete with no wickets. A circle was painted on a length and every ball had to bounce there, a wonderful introduction into the art of bowling.

No other child lived between our house and the school so I walked each way alone. I took the secondary school examination and passed to attend the 'best' secondary school in Swansea, Dynevor Grammar School, which was in the centre of town. All the other boys in the school, including Harry Secombe, went to Swansea Grammar. Yet again I walked back and fore alone.

My father was a cook on a tramp ship carrying coal to Holland. He was a philanderer and treated my mother abominably. He was Walter Edmund and cheated on my mother by taking women on to his ship when in dock. Born and brought up in Liverpool, he was the son of a river pilot. I never knew when he would be home, he just appeared and disappeared in short order, and I was glad to see him go.

My mother was a sweet lady who took in lodgers to earn enough money to live and bring up her two children. Ivy May was a hard worker whom everyone loved. Her men lodgers treated her like the lady she was.

My sister Joan Wilhelmina and I were very different. Joan was the motherly type who would do anything for anyone and who had lots of friends. She constantly looked after me, although I think that on times I resisted her efforts. However she was always there by my side and was a rock in supporting me in family feuds.

One of my mother's lodgers was Ron Challis, a young man working in Cardiff. He took a shine to Joan and courted her and eventually they were married and went to live in his home-town of Dartford, where they still live today. Ron was a skilled engineer and during the war he worked in Scotland on submarines. Joan worked in the Post Office telecommunications department in

Cardiff until they were married. She is still very fond of her little brother.

In Swansea we lived in a small terraced two-storey house, which was next door to the Vicarage on the corner. That was a big posh house and the Vicar and his wife did not mix with us poor folk. Immediately opposite us on the other side of the road was the large St. Thomas Church. However we were not church people so I never went inside. The Methodist Church was some distance away and Joan and I were supposed to go to Sunday school on Sunday afternoons. Joan went but much to Joan's disgust, Ron 'mitched.'

I do not recall how long we lived there but one day my father said that the home-port of the ship was being transferred to Cardiff and that we were moving. The next thing I knew we were living in quite a large house in Canton, a district of West Cardiff.

After a day or two of settling in, my mother took me to Canton High School, which was only about 500 yards away across the main East-to-West road through Cardiff, called Cowbridge Road.

Canton High School was a full block between two roads and was a large attractive building with a large schoolyard in front, which had a boundary wall between it and the pavement. We were guided to the main entrance in the front of the building and directed upstairs. The ground floor was the Girls' school and the boys were up on the first floor. The first floor windows were frosted so that the boys could not look down at the girls in the school playground.

We went upstairs and into a large hall with a big stage at the back and lots of chairs set in rows in the main area where we were greeted by a master who took us to the Headmasters' study, and introduced us to him.

He said 'Welcome Mrs. Warburton, I am Elwyn James, the Headmaster.' He turned to me and said, 'Welcome Ronald, I hope you will be able to come to our school and be very happy.' He then told the master to take me off and show me where my class was, and explain my curriculum and time table.

The master took me out and back through the hall to another corridor with classrooms off to the side. We went into one where a master was sitting at a desk in the front of a class of boys about my age. He introduced me to the other master and left. I gave this master my details and he gave me information on the subjects and a time-table of lessons. He explained every aspect of school life as it affected me, and I was delighted to hear there was a games afternoon every week, Rugby in the winter and Cricket in the summer. He added that the school uniform was compulsory. He then asked if I had any questions, and when I said no, said that I could go find my mother, and come to school the next morning.

The next day we went shopping and bought my new uniform, including games kit, and the school cap, which was a must wear job. The next week was difficult as I knew no one and had to find out where everything was

Then I met a big lad who introduced himself as Bill Ruddock. Bill was the form captain who in the absence of the master, had to control the class. He was captain of the cricket and rugby teams and very friendly. We became firm friends both in and out of school and with his help I joined both the rugby and cricket teams. Cricket was great as I did well, especially at bowling. Initially, I was not so good at Rugby, as the only vacancy was in the forwards. They are traditionally the big fellows and I was a light-weight. Fortunately, the following season I managed to get into the three-quarters, and life was good.

After nine months we moved house and lived in Grangetown, a district in South Cardiff. Once again I had a mile or so to walk to school alone as no one seemed to live near me. One day I was moaning to my mother about my having to walk back and fore and asked if I could have a bike. It was obvious that she had not thought about the distance, and the very next weekend we went out and she bought me a bike. This was a great asset and allowed my friendship with Bill to blossom since he lived so far away. The bike really grew our friendship as we were able to see each other outside of school as well as in.

I was now happier in school than I had ever been and it was reflected in my work as well as on the sports field. I particularly enjoyed mathematics, physics and chemistry. History was a bore and I got into trouble not doing the homework. I also enjoyed art, especially the art master Mr. Bates, called Batty Bates in his absence. He was kind and encouraged me in drawing and elementary painting.

Mr. Bates was a very gentle man and all the boys liked him, so there was no trouble in his class. Under his tutelage my drawing improved dramatically and he seemed to spend a lot of time with me, and it felt that we were friends rather than master and pupil.

'Gussy' Cleal was the physics master and we had a well fitted out physics laboratory. At the end of my fourth year we were in the lab and Gussy said we were going to play with photography equipment and as I was top of the class, my hand was chosen to do the X-ray experiment. It was an old fashioned set up and I had to keep very still for 5 minutes so as not to spoil the photograph. The picture was great and I kept it as a souvenir for a very long time. We had exams at the end of every term and had posh report books in which our results were detailed.

Canton High was particularly interested in boys becoming good swimmers and during the games periods we often went to Cardiff Baths instead of the games field. One afternoon when we arrived at the pool we found that there were a lot of boys from other schools swimming laps with Masters stood on the side counting the lengths. Bill asked what they were doing and was told that they were swimming a mile for a certificate. He asked if he and I could do it and was told 'yes.'

We quickly changed and it was explained that we had to do 75 lengths of the pool for the mile, and 10 lengths extra to allow for the push offs at each end. We had never swum more than 10 lengths in the pool but had done long distances in the sea, so off we went. Up and down the pool we swam and were becoming bored, but neither would give in before the other, so we ended up doing the mile and collected a certificate.

This led us to have a go at swimming point-to-point at Barry Island. Barry Bay is a deep inlet with a large sandy beach. The tide in the Bristol Channel moves very quickly both in and out and whilst when coming in, it is safe to swim far out, when the tide is going out it is easy to be swept out into the channel. Hence, swimming point to point was frowned upon. Many people had drowned attempting the swim, but usually because they were trying to swim it when the tide was going out. We therefore timed our swim accordingly, and did the point-to-point!

We remained good friends until I joined the R.A.F. and Bill joined the army. We only managed one leave together in all our service careers, but our girl friends became very close friends.

My mother's sister, Aunty Rose, lived in Tremorfa and her house backed onto a grassy field known as Cardiff Airport. The field was actually secondary, as it was only a grass facility for aircraft to take off after repairs at Air Despatch Limited. They were a company repairing Hawker biplanes and French Peugeots. My aunt used to 'take in' boarders from this company and once when I was visiting, I met her lodger who was a foreman in one of the hangars. He was a very nice man who talked to me at length about the work they did and the aeroplanes they repaired.

Cardiff was regularly bombed by German aircraft and in early 1941 there was a particularly heavy raid. There was a lot of damage to buildings and housing, and one of the major casualties was Canton High School. When I turned up the next morning, the top floor of the school was missing and the ground floor was still burning. I was sent home obviously and for something to do, went to the airport to see what went on there. I was refused admission at the main gate and it was explained that this was government property and no one was allowed in without a pass.

I went to Aunty Rose's house and found her lodger was in. He asked why I wasn't in school, so I told him about the bombing. He asked what I was going to do and I said I would have to see which other school they would send me to. I said I was not pleased, as I was very happy at Canton.

He must have misunderstood and thought I was asking him to find me a job, because some days later my mother said that she had heard from Aunty Rose's lodger and that if I wanted, an arrangement could be made for me to go to Air Despatch for an interview for a job.

I would have been taking my C.W.B. exams. (Central Welsh Board, the equivalent of the English Matriculation exam) in a couple of months but the thought of working on aeroplanes was too exciting. Also the future of Canton High School seemed to be in some doubt, since it was totally destroyed. In fact, the school was repaired and lasted past the end of the war, until some years later when it was rebuilt.

However, I gladly accepted the offer of having an interview for a job and my friend arranged it. The outcome was that I went for an interview and was offered an apprenticeship, which I readily accepted. Oh, the impatience of youth!

This was an early revelation of a facet of my character that would evidence itself throughout my life: My eagerness to make an early, impetuous decision without thinking it all out. There were times in my R.A.F. career when this was a distinctly advantageous asset. The ability to think quickly and decide between options saved my life on more than one occasion. I must say however, that there were many times in later life when a little prudence would have been beneficial.

Many years later I was elected to Cardiff City Council where it had been agreed to build a new Canton High School to replace the ruined one. I was in the chamber when the motion to discuss the name of the new school came up, and I was able to second the motion to name the school 'Cantonian.' The motion was passed and it is still the name of the school, which now has a long and distinguished history.

CHAPTER 2

APPRENTICE: AIR DESPATCH, LTD.

In April 1941, having been persuaded by me that I was doing the right thing, my Mum cleared it with the Education people and agreed that I could leave school and start work at Air Despatch Ltd. I got out a map of Cardiff and worked out that I could cycle around the north side of Cardiff docks and around the airfield to the east side, the entrance to the works hangars and so get to work easily. I had to begin work at 8 a.m. each day, which meant an early start from home, and I had been advised that I should take sandwiches for lunch. I would not finish until 5.30 p.m. in the evening, so in the winter I would be going and coming home in the dark.

On my arrival the first morning, I was taken to No. 2 hangar to the Works Manager's office and he explained what I would do and what I would be taught. He made it clear that I was a management trainee, and that meant I was there to learn about aircraft and the way they were repaired. He said that working for a living was not like school, time costs money so it was not to be wasted.

I was not, he said, just one of the lads employed as general 'dogsbodies' to the fitters. I was being trained as an apprentice and would work in every part of the factory in turn. The other young lads were good fellows and did a useful job cleaning up and helping the fitters do their job. He then passed me over to the one and only draughtsman employed by the firm who took me on a tour of the whole company. There were two hangars. No.1 was the engine shop and the workshop where aircraft were reconstructed with the parts that had been repaired. In the engine shop they repaired both radial and inline engines.

No. 2 hangar was further around the airport and was where wings and other components were repaired. Some of the biplanes were still covered with fabric, but the modern monoplanes were made entirely of metal.

I was to start in the airframe section and progress through each department until I had acquired a thorough knowledge of the construction of aeroplanes and how they were repaired. On completion of this phase I would pass into the drawing office where I would learn the theoretical and administrative side of the works.

The next day I reported to No. 2 hangar and was taken into the Fabric Shop. This was a very large area, big enough to hold four of the completed aircraft. Wings, rudders and tailplanes of the Hawker biplanes were stripped of their coverings and recovered with pure Irish linen. The wings were on trestles, one could hardly walk between them. It was a sea of cream coloured fabric from wall to wall. Between the wings were women (although we called them ladies back then), from young girls to old ladies (well at my tender 16 years they were old). The men carried the components in and placed them on the trestles. The ladies then stripped the old fabric off and recovered the frames. They sewed all round the edges pulling the fabric very tight.

In order to keep the fabric from ballooning off the frames, cord was passed around each rib of the frame with very long needles and tied off every 3 inches through a linen tape, so there was a double thickness of linen at each rib. The sewing was not my scene so I was put to work on the 'stabbing' as they called it, the cording around the ribs.

The first week in that shop was the most embarrassing of my life. The conversation and the language of these 'ladies' was unbelievable and I was the pit of their jokes. I have never blushed so much before or since. The foreman seemed to think it was a huge joke too, and it wasn't until one of the younger ladies took pity on me and took me under her wing that I had any relief. In a short while I learnt to give, perhaps not as good as I had to take, but at least it was progress.

Almost coincidental with my starting work, the Company opened a new branch in the centre of Cardiff in the large underground garage of a large block of flats in Westgate Street, overlooking Cardiff Arms Park, the home of Glamorgan County Cricket Club.

The Westgate Street branch was divided into two sections, a fabric shop and an airframe and engine maintenance plant. When they transferred me there it was very convenient as it meant a much shorter cycle ride, I saved half an hour on my journey from home to work.

On arrival at the new factory, I was moved into the Dope Shop. This was where the fabric on the wings and tailplanes was coated with a thick red paint known as dope, which as it dried, shrank the fabric. After several coats, the fabric was as tight as a drum, which we frequently played like one, much to the annoyance of the foreman, whose remonstrations seemed to have little effect.

The dope was pungent and not at all pleasant, so everyone wore masks and had to drink a bottle of milk every day, which I never understood. When asked, the foreman merely replied that I should just enjoy it. I was later told that the milk would form a lining on the stomach and prevent harm done by the inhalation of the dope fumes.

When the fabric shrinkage reached a satisfactory stage the surfaces were sprayed in camouflage—brown and green—and when dry, the units were taken either to No. 1. hangar at the airport, or loaded onto lorries and taken to other repair depots for assembly.

Luckily my sojourn in this department was brief and I moved on to the metal shop, filled with assorted parts of airframes, fuselages, wings, tailplanes, and engine parts, all in various stages of repair and assembly.

When Westgate Street opened, a new general manager was appointed and a short while after he called me into the office and told me that he was going to put me with the best fitters and that I was not to mess about but to knuckle down and learn. He said that I was a management trainee and that offered a good future for me.

At this time I was earning £1.10, one pound, ten shillings per week, which to an ex-school-boy was a lot of money. My father emphasized the point and told me to give my Mum half for my 'keep.' Bill Ruddock was still in school at this time and being a wise chap, he took his C.W.B exams and passed them all. We still met at weekends but as I had left school I could not play rugby for the team, but I did go along and watch.

At Air Despatch there was a wide range of ages, men and boys. I was amazed to see some very old chaps, some over 80 years of age, who had volunteered to go back to work to help the war effort. It was amazing to see how skillful they still were, slow perhaps, but the quality of their work was excellent.

Most of the men were highly skilled and worked very hard, but it was again uncomfortable for me to hear the dreadful language. I found it strange that such skillful men were so badly spoken and lacking in education. However, they were good to me, the humour a little crude perhaps, but they were pleased to show me how things should be done. The most elderly of them was the sweeper up, tea boy and general factotum, who was eighty years old if he was a day, and known to everyone as 'Old Bill.'

We started at 8 a.m. with tea breaks at 10 a.m. and 3:30 p.m., when we sat around a great big coke stove in the middle of the factory on boxes and planks drinking tea and eating sandwiches of all descriptions. Due to the rationing of food, there was no meat, so it was fish paste or jam.

Poor old Bill was teased constantly, usually about sex and the implication was that he was too old for it (but not put quite as politely as that). Bill used to get embarrassed and in the end would say he could still do it if he wanted to. I thought this was very cruel and my comments (innocent and naïve) in defense of Bill made matters worse and caused great laughter. There were other boys working in the metal shop, their ages varying from 14 to 16, and I found them extremely difficult to get along with. I presumed this was because of our different standards of education. They had left poor schools in the docks area, whilst I was a grammar school boy.

I recall being put to work with the jig maker and was shown how to file a block of steel accurately with a steel file. It was a very difficult task, keeping the file dead flat so that it did not round the edges, so that the surface remained absolutely level. This was really before I was capable of doing the job satisfactorily.

I was put to making a blanking tool for locking tabs. On an aircraft every fastener has to have a locking device, and tabs were used to lock the nuts on fixing bolts. I was having great difficulty in getting the top of the block dead flat. I thought I was very clever when I rubbed it on an oil stone instead of filing it. This was the worst thing I could have done, as it was impossible to make it flat that way. Unfortunately for me I was caught in the act, and for the first time, I had a real dressing down by the manager.

It was beneficial in the end because it made me knuckle down and do my work properly and responsibly. I had worked in the metal shop for about six months when one day I was called into the Works Manager's office. I went with fear and trepidation. I was sure I had done something wrong and was on the carpet. The Works Manager was a mature and very skilful tradesman, with long experience in the trade. He was a tall, thin man, and was very particular in his dress. Although he was working on the shop floor, he was extremely clean.

Much to my amazement, he was very friendly and said that I had made a very good start, and that I had made a lot of progress. He then said that in future I would be spending two days a week in the drawing office to learn about plans and drawings.

He took me into the drawing office and left me with the draughtsman, whose name I cannot remember, but who was very friendly. The draughtsman asked me how I was enjoying the work in the factory, and I told him it was all a bit bewildering. I said I was a bit conscious of the different treatment I was receiving compared to the other lads.

He explained to me that all the others had left school at 14 and that theirs was not at all like the school I had gone to. He said they naturally resent you. If you want to get along with them treat them as equals, be friendly towards them. What a lesson for a 16 year old! I don't think I fully appreciated it at the time but it certainly paid dividends later.

My days in the drawing office were fascinating and informative and gradually became more frequent. I was not only taught to read drawings, but to understand how they were laid out, and later I learnt the technical descriptions of projections. I found out how they were copied for the workshop and how to draw to scale. I was so lucky in my draughtsman teacher; he was not only patient but seemed to enjoy the teaching and did far more than was the original intention.

I used to spend my lunchtime breaks with him and our conversations were wide-ranging and wonderful. We talked about all sorts of things, such as home life, education and sport. He was a very nice man about thirty, married with children, and he treated me extremely well.

CHAPTER 3

THE R.A.F BECKONS

The draughtsman and I were having lunch together in the office on a Friday late in September 1943, when I confessed my burning desire to fly with the R.A.F., and to my surprise, this was received with enthusiasm. He pointed out that being almost 18, I would probably be called up soon anyway, so why not volunteer? He explained that it took nearly 12 months to train for aircrew, so one could get in before one's 18th birthday. He knew all this because he had tried to join but had failed the aircrew medical.

That was all I needed, and the next day found me at the R.A.F. Recruitment office in Windsor Place in the centre of Cardiff, where I was cordially received and given forms to fill out. I waited around for a while and then was called in to see an officer, who went through the forms and asked what I was doing at present. I explained where I worked, and what I did. He suggested I apply to be a flight engineer as I was at least part of the way there, and it would take less time to train than being a pilot. He said there was a very long waiting list for pilots and with my work experience I would be readily accepted for training as a flight engineer.

So that was it, and the forms went off!

Afterwards, I was very grateful to that officer, because had I insisted on being a pilot I would not have finished my training before the war ended, and certainly not in time for active service. However, I heard nothing for a while (ages it seemed to me). I pestered the recruiting office, both on the phone and going in during my lunch hour. Finally, to pacify me, the officer there said he would see if I could join the University Air Squadron. This was a means of training university students waiting for their call up for aircrew training, and gave preliminary instruction in Morse Code communication and various other helpful matters. Although I was not at university, I was somehow accepted, and spent two evenings a week there until I was conversant with wireless communication through Morse Code.

After six weeks, I could actually send and read Morse Code at 15 words a minute, the required standard. At first I had found it very difficult, but after a couple of weeks it suddenly registered, and I found I could send and receive at the required speed.

After three years in Air Despatch I was ready for the R.A.F., I thought. I received an official communication one day, but it was not my call up papers, it was a directive to report to F. N. Morgan & Co. in City Road, Cardiff to work on the repairing of Bostons (American twin-engine bombers). I showed the letter to my superiors at Air Despatch and they were very upset. They protested to the R.A.F., stating that my training was far better put to use where I was than in a small garage only repairing small parts. However, it had no effect, so I had to go to work in the garage.

When I started, there was only one chap in the section allocated to the repairs of the stub wings, and the space could only accommodate two wings at a time. The man's name was Jim, and he was a very nice fellow, but in fact he knew very little about aircraft, as he was a garage fitter. It fell to me to explain about the effects of dissimilar metal corrosion and how one had to use Durellac between the surfaces.

One day an inspector came to examine the facilities and the 'factory.' He very quickly assessed the situation, and said that the repairing contract was cancelled. I asked what was I to do and he said that as I would be called up shortly I should remain with F. N. Morgan and learn about car engines which were akin to aero engines, only smaller. For the next few weeks, after being taught to drive, I worked on cars.

Fortunately, I did not have to wait too long before the postman delivered a letter from the R.A.F., but it was still not the call up I expected, it was a note to report to Penarth R.A.F. Medical Centre for an Aircrew Medical. This would last two days. The letter also stated that as I resided in the area, I should travel back and forth each day.

I had the longest and most intensive medical examination of all the parts of my body! There were also various tests including intelligence papers.

The eye tests were particularly severe and after the normal eye chart where one reads the letters, I was sat in front of a long box with a top hiding the interior. The end nearest to me had a slot so I could look down the length of the inside. There were two long rails carrying a vertical stem on each. On the front of the box was a wheel which when turned moved the stems so that they moved in conjunction with each other but in opposite directions. I was told to line the stems up by turning the wheel and found that as I did so, the stems moved back and fore in relation to each other. It quickly dawned that they would be the same height when in line but looking horizontally at the same level of the stems made it extremely difficult. I was told to experiment for a few moments and then told, 'Line them up.' Apparently I did, because I passed and moved on to the next test.

I moved to a table where a chap in a white coat sat with a chair alongside him and indicated for me to sit down. On the table between us was a book about 8" x 6" and very thick. He opened the cover and the page on the right was like embroidery with a number set in the middle in a contrasting colour. He said I was to turn each page and call out the numbers. It was easy at first, but as I progressed the colours merged until it was a matter of merely shades of difference. This test was made difficult as so many applicants were colour-blind. I was told that I had passed all the eyesight tests and could proceed to the next test.

The various tests continued until I wondered if there was any part of me they had not checked. I was directed to yet another building and then had what would now be termed Mensa tests. At the end of the second day I was told that I had passed all tests, was fit to train as aircrew, and would receive my joining up papers very soon. It was indeed very soon, as on the 21st January, 1944 I was summoned to report at the Aircrew Reception Centre at St. John's Wood in London.

My Mum fussed over me asking what I needed and making suggestions of what to take with me. I told her the R.A.F. only wanted me and would give me everything I needed. On the due date I caught a train from Cardiff direct to Paddington and a bus to Regents Park.

Chapter 4

I JOIN THE R.A.F

Adjacent to the Regents Canal in Regents Park were luxury blocks of flats, and to my surprise on one was a large board saying:

AIRCREW RECEPTION CENTRE

From outside the building they appeared to be luxury flats, but the inside and furnishings were certainly not. I went into the door labeled 'OFFICE' and received a cordial greeting from a W.A.A.F. sat at a desk. She asked me my name, and I obliged, and was invited to sit down in front of her. She looked at her list and said, 'O.K. you're one of the early ones, so you'll have your pick. Go along to the next door and go up to the first floor. All the four rooms are the same and you can take your pick of the beds, alongside which there will be a cupboard to put your coat and clothes in.'

She explained that there was a canteen/dining room in the basement of the building where we would have our meals and also a N.A.A.F.I. She said that we would find these wherever we went as they were like a shop for us to buy whatever we needed on R.A.F. Property. It was also a bar where could get all kinds of drinks and snacks. She said that we were free for the evening and to report outside the building at 8 a.m. tomorrow morning on the pavement.

I went next door and up to the room to find I was the first to arrive. Everywhere there were bare boards and the rooms were full of two-tier metal bunks and steel cupboards. I picked a bed and put my bag in the cupboard. After about an hour two more chaps came in and we introduced ourselves. We sorted ourselves out and then went down to the basement and had our first meal in the R.A.F. It was bulk cooking and we sat at trestle tables but I was agreeably surprised at the quality of the food. Afterwards we returned to our room and had an early night.

The first morning after our arrival we were assembled in the road outside the flats, told to get into three ranks and marched up to Lords Cricket Ground. Under one of the stands was a store and inside against the back wall was a large counter with a hatch over. In the hatch space were three airmen and we lined up to pass them one at a time. As we approached the first airman called out, 'Chest size' and when we gave this, clothes appeared like magic. Uniforms, underclothes, a great coat, boots and socks, and a forage cap, everything an airman required.

Fortunately, the first item we received was a white kit bag and all the garments were quickly 'stuffed' in as we were hastened along the line. Undergarments, such as socks were in threes: one on, one in the wash, and one clean. We even had a pair of woolen gloves and a towel.

Then with very heavy, full bags on our shoulders, we were marched around to a clinic. There we had our 'jabs', inoculations against typhoid, and every other disease imaginable, plus a vaccination. We were then marched back to Regents Park and told to go and get properly dressed and then fall in for inspection.

We went up to our rooms where we put all our civvy kit in the locker, a small metal cupboard with three shelves and some hanging space. We unpacked our kit bags and donned our uniforms, most of which fitted very well, somewhat surprisingly, given the allocation process. The real pleasure for us all was to take the small piece of snow-white cotton and place it in the front of our forage caps. We were so proud of that white flash that indicated to everyone that we were training to be aircrew.

We went downstairs and stood in three lines in the road and suddenly there appeared an aging Warrant Officer, complete with cane and very loud voice. He proceeded to tell us that we were Cadets and that we were a long way from being airmen, but that he would make a good start at teaching us.

He then started walking down the line, inspecting each cadet, yelling loudly at all items he did not like. Apparently, he did not like anything he saw. Amazingly he didn't even get hoarse. He stopped in front of me.

"When did you shave last Cadet?" he yelled.

"Last Wednesday," I replied. Talk about an idiot!

He was speechless for a very brief moment, and then he screamed, "YOU are in the Air Force now, and you will bloody well shave everyday, whether you need it or not! Understand?" I understood.

For 14 days he marched us up and down, round and round until we were shattered. We did marching and rifle drill until we dropped. We were insulted in ways we had never imagined possible. There was no going out at night. We were lucky to have enough energy to climb the stairs back up to our double-decker bunks.

On the 15th morning, the 6th February 1944, we were told to pack and be back down in seconds, we had a train to catch.

So off we went in lorries to Paddington Station, boarded a train and finished up in Newquay, Cornwall, after a weary train journey of 7 hours, stopping at every station between London and Cornwall. We were billeted in the Beaconsfield Hotel right on the esplanade. This was the Initial Training Wing, and their job was to teach us the discipline and basic skills required by the R.A.F.

We learnt about Lee Enfield rifles and Sten guns, and had to score a pass on the rifle range with live ammunition. For six weeks we drilled and had lectures. One day we were taken to the cinema. Expecting a film on flying training or something similar, we were somewhat shocked when an Officer appeared on the stage and told us about the dangers of Venereal Disease and unprotected sex.

I don't think more than about 5 per cent of us young lads had ever had sex but we certainly learnt about it that day. Then the lights dimmed and the film started. First it showed the initial stages of various diseases and then got down to the nitty gritty.

I have never seen anything before or since that was so horrible: technicolour pictures of infected skin and privates and within minutes people were passing out, and being sick. If the intention was to put us off sex, then they certainly succeeded, if only for a short while.

I have happy memories of Newquay because we had relatively comfortable rooms, the food was good, and I started to make real friends. Our working day was not too long and we had every weekend free. It was cold but the weather was nice and so we could walk on the beach and the esplanade, play football, but no rugby. There was a cafe at the beach which spoilt us with cheap tea and buns, and we spent hours playing draughts and chess.

Little did I know that many years later Margaret and I would spend our honeymoon there.

Initial Training Wing for Aircrew, Newquay, March, 1945.

On the 3rd March 1944 we boarded a train to Bristol, where we changed trains for one to Cardiff. This was my home town, but we only changed platforms and got on a train to St. Athan.

CHAPTER 5

FLIGHT ENGINEER'S SCHOOL

We proceeded to our next stage, which was to the Flight Engineer's School at St. Athan, near Cardiff. This was a peace-time aerodrome with lovely buildings of brick and block construction and big brick construction hangars. Our accommodations were in barrack blocks but they were very comfortable, with linoleum flooring and we had beds for the first time instead of double-decker bunks. The beds still had metal frames, but they were proper beds with a mattress and even a pillow. There were about twenty of us in all, divided into two classes. We were told that one class would start in the airframe shop and the other would start in the engine shop. After completion of that part of our training we would swap over.

The next morning we were marched over to a large hangar big enough to hold three Lancasters, and separated into two sections. One section consisted of a series of class areas with blackboards in front and seating at desks with about six to each class facing the blackboard.

The rest of the area had portions of airframes and fuselages. At the rear was a Lancaster, the aeroplane I longed to fly in. This was my first sight of this beautiful aircraft. I was so delighted for I had feared I would get put onto Halifaxes or Stirlings.

The Lancaster had quickly earned a reputation for being a superb aircraft that was very maneuverable. It carried the biggest bomb load of any aircraft.

We were divided up into two classes of five and took our places at the desks, where we found ourselves face to face with our instructors. Ours was a corporal, with whom we would spend the next few months. I looked at the Corporal and he looked at me and said, "Hello Warburton."

I said "Hello Mr. Bates." It was my old art master from Canton High School!

He reminded me gently that he was Corporal Bates now. I always thought Mr. Bates was a nice man at school, but I learnt that he was an exceptional teacher and a very good friend. His advice was invaluable and he protected me from so many silly errors. He was also an excellent instructor. His diagrams of the various systems, such as hydraulics and fuel, were masterpieces, beautifully drawn and coloured.

The first thing we did was to go to the full body of the Lanc and climb up inside. I was so keen I raced the others and was stood by the door, which was about 5 foot high just in front of the tail plane. As we entered I was struck by the darkness. It did not dawn on me that it would not be illuminated inside. There was no lining to the framing and everything was dark green. It was like going into a tunnel, about 6 feet high and 5 feet wide.

Immediately above our heads was the mid-upper turret, a Perspex dome with two Browning machine guns sticking up, and a seat suspended down. My immediate reaction was that I would not like to sit on that for any length of time. To the rear was an 'Elsan,' a toilet, but it was really more like an oil drum. Behind that was the rear turret with four Browning machine guns.

I turned back and made my way forward and at the end of this part of the fuselage there was a barrier. This was a flat sheet of metal blocking half of the fuselage, extending up about 2 feet and which we had to clamber over. It turned out to be the rear main wing spar, and the end paneling of the bomb bay. There was a recess of five feet between it and the front main spar.

In the recess, on the left hand side was a large chest-like box with an upholstered bed on top. I turned to the guy behind me and said, 'Looks like we get a kip on long trips,' only to get a tittering laugh. Corporal Bates carefully set us straight, 'That is for the wounded and dying, I don't think you'll want to use that.'

When we climbed over the front spar we passed through a curtain to the main cabin with a passage down the right hand side. Immediately on the left was a small seat with a huge wireless set in front forming a barrier half way across the fuselage.

Behind the wireless operator's table was a table and seat, which was the navigator's area. Then, on the left built up off the floor was the pilot's seat with the control column in front and rudder bar underneath. This seat, like the two gunners' seats, was recessed. Those three had parachutes of the old-fashioned type, which had a harness over the shoulders, so they were sitting on them all the time. The rest of us had separate harnesses, which we wore all the time. In an emergency we took a parachute off a rack, and clipped it onto our chest.

In the middle was the consol with the four throttles on top, the levers for the propellers below and below them the flap controls. The instrument panel extended right across the plane. There was a Perspex canopy above, extending from the instrument panel right back to the wireless operator's spot, finishing in an astral dome. It was just like a glass house and the visibility was superb.

I asked, 'Where is the engineer's seat?' and was shown a canvas strip hanging down on the right. That clipped onto the consol, and that strap was what you might swing on for up to 9 hours. Nice and comfy! I don't think. It was better than a long stand though.

In front of the engineer's position and below the instrument panel was a large square hole, which led down into the nose, which was occupied by the bomb aimer. He had more room and comfort than anyone else, as the floor was upholstered to form a couch, and he was able to lie down full length. Above this area was the front gun turret with two guns.

We climbed back out and went on a tour of the rest of the airframe department, looking at diagrammatic boards of circuits and systems. Back at our class area, Corporal Bates said that the next morning we would start the serious business of learning everything about the Lancaster.

The next day commenced a period of intense instruction on all the systems and the construction of the Lancaster. We followed the routes of all the controls and learnt how they were operated. We learnt about hydraulics, pneumatics, electrics, and fuel systems and what their functions were. We spent quite some time on what to do in emergencies when damage occurred, and ways and means of operating when the systems were out of action.

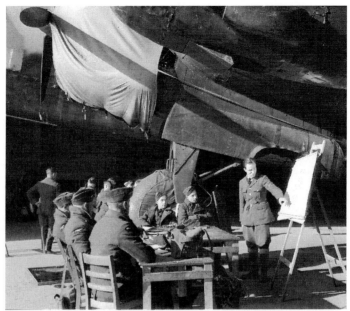

Flight Engineers undergoing intensive training at St Athan by experienced ground instructors. (Photograph with permission, Imperial War Museum. CH. 12467.)

We spent every day and Saturday mornings in class and Saturday afternoons were for sports or P.T. Saturday night was the free night when we could leave camp and go to Cardiff to a dance, or more likely the pub. Sunday was a free day after Church parade, which was avoided if possible.

This part of the course lasted just over three months, until mid June 1944. We had an oral and a written examination and then sweated for two days until the results were posted on the notice board. The results said simply 'passed' or 'failed', along with an indication that those who had failed could re-muster for training as air gunners. It was said that this was the way the R.A.F.

recruited gunners, as no one in their right mind would volunteer for that job!

I had passed!

Most of my friends had also passed, but I was very surprised that three had failed out of the ten.

Studying the Lancaster's hydraulics and controls. (Photograph with permission, Imperial War Museum. CH. 12472.)

During this period of the course I had built up a friendship with a guy called Arthur, who was in the bed next to me and hailed from Merthyr Tydfil. He was an ex-Grammar school lad and was very bright. He asked one day if I liked classical music and I confessed I had never listened to any. He said there was a music club on site on Wednesday evenings when a Sergeant talked about the music and then played recordings. He asked if I would like to try it and I readily agreed. This was the start of my great love of music, and I have forever been grateful to him. We did not miss one session while we were there.

Flight Engineers learning about the Lancaster. (Photograph, Imperial War Museum. CH. 12473.)

The following Monday we started on engines in the other half of the hangar, with a similar layout, but without Corporal Bates. Our instructor this time was not nearly as nice. He was what we called a 'time serving type,' which usually meant an attitude toward aircrew trainees. The airmen who were in the Air Force prior to the war were inclined to be a bit superior to the wartime volunteers.

We were faced with a large Merlin engine on a cradle and there was one engine for every two trainees. We were lectured at first on the construction and all the components. We then had to totally strip it down and reassemble it, and there was trouble if you had a bit left over.

Then we moved to another bay and started all over again on a Pratt & Whitney radial engine. It was necessary to be familiar with both types of engine as some Lancasters were being made in Canada and those were fitted with the radial engine. Once again there was emphasis on damage control and emergency measures.

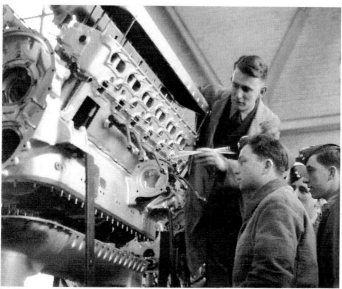

A thorough knowledge of engines was essential for every Flight Engineer and was a high priority in training. (Photograph with permission, Imperial War Museum. CH. 12466.)

After completing the engine phase, we were on to propellers with variable pitch, and learnt the full details of operating and functions. Much emphasis was placed on the necessity for fuel economy. We were told that the purpose of our mission was to deliver the maximum bomb load to the target, and so fuel was calculated for the trips with very little to spare. More fuel meant fewer bombs.

However, our joy was short lived: we had to face a final written paper and oral test, which took a whole day. Each cadet had an individual examiner for the oral in the morning and it seemed that we were being tested on more than our knowledge of the technicalities, but with situation problems. It was an endeavour to see how we would react in an emergency. In the afternoon we had a written examination.

Even during off-hours we studied the boards. (Photograph with permission, Imperial War Museum. CH. 12470.)

We then sweated for two days until the results were posted. We had marks this time and they were out of a 1,000. Marks over 700 merited a recommendation for a commission and only two people achieved this.

We learnt that the large main fuel tanks were in the areas of the wings between the fuselage and the outer engines. There were reserve tanks in the areas of the wings beyond the outer engines and these had to be emptied into the main tanks for the fuel to be used. We also learnt of the fire extinguisher system fitted to each engine nacelle (housing) together with details of where the fire extinguishers were in the plane. Despite the lack of friendliness, our instructor must have taught us well, as all of us passed the examinations.

Flight Engineers undergoing individual oral examination by senior instructors. (Photograph with permission, Imperial War Museum. CH. 12471.)

I scored 699. I was a little despondent and moped about until Mr. Bates sought me out, and we went for a pint of beer together. He congratulated me, but I said I was disappointed.

He said that there were comments on my papers that said I was too young and immature for recommendation for a commission, so I was marked down for that reason, but that my actual marks put me above the rest. It was on my record that I was top of the course, with the comments stating why the marks were reduced.

We had a formal passing out parade on 21st September, 1944, after we had proudly sewn on our engineers brevet, the half-wing worn above the left breast pocket, and the sergeant's stripes on each arm. We were as proud as could be.

The Flight Engineer's brevet.

No more white flashes in our caps. We were proper R.A.F. at last!

We were given seven days leave, and I went home to Cardiff. For the entire time, I didn't go out in anything except my R.A.F. uniform. I have to say that I have never had so much success with girls at dances, and had the time of my life.

Proudly displaying the Flight Engineer's brevet on my left breast and my Sergeant's Stripes, upon graduation from Flight School, September, 1944.

CHAPTER 6

FLYING!

I had been told to report direct to the Elementary Flying School near Oxford at the end of my leave, and this was a week of heaven. Only two others were with me on this posting so it was very personal. We did nothing but fly around in Oxfords and Ansons, both twin-engine aircraft, just learning about flying in general with an occasional go at the controls.

There was one course not on flying aircraft, but learning how to use a parachute. We started in a hangar jumping off towers which got higher and higher, learning to roll as we hit the ground. Then we were taken up by a barrage balloon, stood in a basket, wearing a 'chute' and suddenly told to jump. The ground looked a long way down and I did not like this at all.

There were many cries of 'I wish I hadn't joined' but the N.C.O lost patience and we had to jump. It was fine once the chute opened but the ground came up much faster than I had been led to believe and I hit with a crunch that jarred my bones and scared me to death. However, there were no lasting effects and at least we knew a parachute worked.

The next day we went up in an Anson and had to do a proper jump. This time my jump went smoothly, and although it was still a bit of a bump, at least I was prepared this time.

We had a couple more days of flying and then were told that we were posted. The three of us were posted to Bottesford, an aerodrome 20 miles east of Nottingham, a Heavy Conversion Unit, where the crews who had been training on twin-engine aircraft were moved up to four-engine aircraft. The six man crews were increased to seven by the addition of a flight engineer. We were given travel warrants and off we went the next day.

I arrived at Bottesford on the 10th December 1944. There were five of us engineers and we were not allowed any time to settle in. The next morning we had to report to Hangar No. 1, where we found five crews stood in line with the pilots at the front. We were told by a Flight Lieutenant (F/Lt.) to stand in a line in front of and facing the crews.

I noticed that on the end of the line of crews was a crew of four English and two Australians, who stood out in their navy blue uniforms. The pilot in front was an officer, an Australian, and the only officer in the whole body of trainees. The F/Lt. told the pilots, 'O.K. Chaps, go get yourself an engineer.'

The pilots left the groups and came over and started chatting to us individually. The first guy who came to me was a sergeant pilot with a Scottish accent who I did not like, nor apparently did he like me, because he moved on quickly. Then the Australian Pilot Officer came up to me and asked me a few questions, and then he looked at a list and said, 'What did you say your name was?' I said 'Warburton, Sir.'

He said, 'Let's go over there out of this mob and have a chat.' This we did, and he asked a lot of personal questions and then quite suddenly asked, 'Would you like to fly with me?' I said, 'Yes,' and so we went to join the rest of his crew. He introduced himself to me saying, 'My name is Alf Cowley, you don't have to call me 'Sir' unless we are in a formal situation. Otherwise, call me Alf.' He seemed much older than the other pilots who were all young sergeants.

I was extremely self-conscious and at sea in this situation. I was also conscious of the fact that he was an officer and that I was a very young and inexperienced engineer. However, I think Alf sensed this and smiled and said 'Let me introduce you to the rest of the crew.' We walked over to the others and he introduced me, 'Lads, he said, 'This is Ron Warburton, our Flight Engineer.' Then turning to the others he said, 'This is Charlie Lane, he's our navigator.' Charlie was in his mid-twenties, as far as I could tell, but obviously older than me, and quite tall.

Turning to the other Australian he said, 'This is Mac McGair, he's our wireless operator.' Mac was shorter than Charlie, about my height, and very fair. He just said, 'Hello.' Alf then turned to a short stout fellow who was considerably older than the rest and said 'This is Pete Green, he is the rear gunner.' Pete just said 'Hi' and shook my hand. Alf then turned to a shorter fellow who was not so stout and said, 'This is Bob Davies, he is the bomb aimer.' Bob also shook my hand and said, 'Hello.' The last of the crew was a quiet, almost dour chap of about twenty, and Alf said he was the mid-upper gunner, Ian McKenzie.

Alf then said that we should go to the mess and get acquainted over a cup of tea, so we all trooped out and he led the way to the Sergeants' Mess. I formed the opinion that Alf was so much older than all the others and seemed so much in charge. The other sergeant pilots were much younger and more immature.

On the way to the mess Alf explained that normally, as an officer, he would not be allowed in the Sergeant's Mess, but today was an exception and it was O.K. We entered a large Nissen hut and the entrance hall was quite large with a table against the side wall.

Above the table was a large black board with white lettering. On top was '1668 Heavy Conversion Unit, Bottesford.' Underneath was, 'Flying Programme,' with a table of horizontal and vertical lines. The top consisted of the headings for the columns, Date, Pilot, Navigator, etc., then Exercise No. and Take-off Time. Below was a series of lines for the data to be inserted.

Alf said, 'You have to read this board early every morning to find out what we are doing.' Then he turned to me and said, 'That is for you, as all the others are used to it from our previous training.' We then went into a large and very well furnished lounge with settees, arm chairs and tables in the front section and behind that area was a large well stocked bar. At the side of the bar was a large doorway into a dining room. On the left were trestle tables for about ten and on the right a large table, behind which was a big hatch with a kitchen behind.

Alf led us to a table in the lounge with chairs around and we all sat down. He then gave me a brief description of each member of the crew's tasks in the aircraft. Then he told the others what my role was. After a brief discussion, he rose and said he would see us all in the briefing room tomorrow morning, and left.

Bob said, 'Let's go to the billet and get Ron settled', so I picked up my kitbag and followed them out, and we walked along to the billets, which were large Nissen huts made of corrugated steel, semi circular in shape with windows in the sides. We passed a few then went into the next and there were single metal framed beds with blankets folded on the head end and COTTON SHEETS folded on top, also a pillow with a COTTON pillow case.

Bob looked at my face, which must have registered my surprise and said, 'We all did that at Flying School. It's a perk for Aircrew.'

There were only seven beds in the hut and again Bob said, 'Another perk, each crew has their own hut.' I dropped my bag on an empty bed, and opened the locker beside the bed. It was quite a bit larger than those I had had before and so it was easy to unpack and put my clothes and kit away. Bob seemed to be the friendly one, because he was really looking after me. He said, 'Let me show you the toilet block' and we went over the road to a wooden hut opposite, which had showers down the front side, and toilets opposite.

We went back into the hut and Charlie said we should go and have lunch, so we all trooped off to the mess. The lunch was better than anything I had had in the Air Force to date, and I think it showed as Pete said, 'One of the perks of being aircrew is we get good grub.'

After lunch we sat in the lounge for a while and I was delighted that they all joined in and talked of what they had done at the elementary flying school. They were unanimous in praising Alf's ability as a pilot, but said he was a hard task-master and you really had to perform.

The next morning when we went to the mess and found our names on the top of the board, and we were to do Exercise 1, Familiarisation.

The names were all there and I was pleased to see on the end underneath Flight Engineer was 'Sgt. Warburton.'

Briefing time was 9 a.m. We had breakfast and went to the briefing room where we found Alf already there. On the back wall was a large map of England with a small area of the French coast on the bottom. In front of the map was a platform with a table and chairs behind.

It was quite a large room and the area in front of the table was filled with tables, each with seven chairs. Alf was sat at one of the tables near the front so we joined him. He said, 'Good morning, have a seat and pay attention.' Hardly had he finished when two Officers came into the room and went to the front table. They were both Flight Lieutenants with pilot's wings. One stood up and said, 'Good morning, I am Flight Lieutenant Ken Major, Chief Training Officer and I will be supervising your training.'

The five crews were all present, they separated and each chose a table and we were spread over the area as if we had an infectious disease. F/Lt. Major continued saying 'You will start today with a lecture of sorts at dispersal where you will meet your personal training officer, each crew has its own.' He then read out five officers' names and ours was Flying Officer (F/O) Reeves. He said, 'They will be here shortly and will take you to the dispersal where you will commence your training.'

'After your familiarization you will move on to circuits and landings until your training officer is satisfied. When he thinks you are ready, during long cross-country flights you will do exercises replicating bombing, fighter affiliation, and searchlight evasion. You will also do group exercises, where you will practice formation flying until you have mastered the art of flying very close together in safety.'

The Lancaster Bomber. The "HA" denotes 218 (Gold Coast) Squadron, and the "U" on the nose shows this to be the legendary HA/U (Uncle). The white stripes on the tail denote the flight leader.

'Your days will consist of lectures in here and flying exercises until we are satisfied that you have reached the standard necessary to go to a squadron. Good Luck.'

He sat down and as he did so five Flying Officers came in and found their trainee crews and joined them. Ours was in his late twenties, I think, and he came straight over to us and introduced himself, Flying Officer Reeves. He said, 'Hello chaps, let's go to the stores and get you kitted out.'

We went out and walked around to a building behind the others and went inside. F/O Reeves introduced us as Alf Cowley's crew and asked the stores assistant to fit us out with flying kit. We stood in line behind Alf and were issued with a soft leather flying helmet complete with goggles and oxygen mask, a white long sleeved pullover, and flying boots.

It was explained that this was our personal kit and we would retain it all while we were flying. Other kit like flying suits and parachutes we would get each day as required for that particular exercise. The boots were special. They were black shoes at the bottom, with fleece lining up to the top of the calf. It was explained that in the fleece was a pocket containing a pen-knife, which would be used if shot down to make them like ordinary shoes, by cutting off the tops.

We went outside and there was a lorry waiting and we all climbed in the back whilst F/O Reeves went in the front. The lorry took us out to dispersal, where three Lancasters were parked. He said we are working on 'J. Johnny' this morning.

F/O Reeves explained that each aircraft had its own code of three letters. For example, 'HA/U' would indicate the squadron (HA) and the aircraft (U). These were painted in very large letters on each side of the fuselage near the door and in small letters at the nose by the nose cone. When flying in formation if anything happened to an adjacent aircraft, on our return we would be able to report what we had seen and to which plane. With the reports of all the aircraft in the formation, the security officers could build up a picture of everything that happened on the raid.

He led us around to the second Lancaster and we stood looking up at the nose. He said that we should climb aboard and familiarize ourselves with our positions. He then turned to me and said that as I was already familiar with the aircraft, I should go over to the maintenance hut and talk to 'Chiefy,' who was in charge of the three aircraft in this flight, and on my return, he would be pleased to show me the pre-flight checks applicable to me.

I went off to the maintenance hut and found a Flight Sergeant sitting inside at a dirty old desk. I went in and very nervously said, 'Excuse me Chiefy, I'm supposed to have a chat with you, but actually I don't have a clue what to say.' He laughed and said that I was not to worry, everyone has to learn, engineering school is one thing but being on an aerodrome is very different.

Chiefy took me by the arm and marched me to the aircraft. We walked around the aircraft and he showed me the locking devices on the controls, emphasizing that it was my job to see that they had been removed. He said it was his job to remove them but stressed my part in the responsibility of seeing it had been done.

Then in a kindly manner he emphasized that my relationship with the ground crew was extremely important. He said our lives depended on their maintenance and if there were good relations they would take an interest in our welfare and take care of us.

I returned to the aircraft and we were invited to climb in and look around, especially at where we each would operate. I waited until last and then made my way up into the cockpit area and stood by the consol. It was a very different feeling to St. Athan; this was not an aircraft in a hangar but the aircraft we would fly. Alf was already in the pilot's seat and smiled at me and said 'You don't have a seat, hard luck.'

After we had a good look around we got out of the aircraft and F/O Reeves smilingly asked if everyone was O.K. We all agreed and he said, 'Let's get back and you can relax for the rest of the morning. After lunch you start in earnest with familiarization exercises. Thereafter you will gradually progress through the programme of day and night flying with bombing practice and fighter affiliation.'

We were dismissed for the rest of the morning. After lunch we had a brief talk in the Briefing Room and went straight to the dispersal with F/O Reeves. He picked me out and said I should do the checks that were my responsibility prior to flight.

He said the locking devices on all the controls had been removed but I needed to be very familiar with all of them and where they were as well as the cover of the Pitot head. This was the device for determining our speed and conveying it to the speedometer in the instrument panel. I walked around the aircraft 'J. Johnny', and found that all the locking devices were removed and also the Pitot head cover. I climbed into the aircraft to find the instructor in the pilot's seat and Alf standing where I would have stood. F/O Reeves said, 'You have to take a back seat for the first few goes but don't worry, your turn will come.'

Since Alf was standing where I was expected to, I stood behind him. F/O Reeves opened the side window and shouted down to the ground crew, 'Ready to start engines.' The throttle levers on the top of the consol are shaped, with the two centre ones vertical and the two outer ones turned over the top of the inners. When taxiing, this enables the pilot or engineer to move the two outers easily independent of the inners.

The signal came from below and he pressed the starter for the port outer. I knew this was the one with the charging unit that charged the batteries and had to be started first. There was a wheeled ground accumulator unit under the aircraft for starting the engines so that the heavy power load required to start the engine would not flatten the aircraft's internal batteries.

The engines were all started up and I was like a lost sheep. Alf was standing in my place and there was very little space for me. Added to which he was doing my job!

When the engines were running F/O Reeves waved his hands to the ground crew and yelled, 'Chocks away.' The next thing I knew we were taxiing out of dispersal and moving along the perimeter track, which we always referred to as the 'peri track.' There was a constant stream of conversation between F/O Reeves and Alf and I was taking in every word.

We turned around and returned to the dispersal where Alf and F/O Reeves changed places. Then Alf took the aircraft around the peri track.

Suddenly F/O Reeves said to me, 'Right, up you come,' and he moved back around me, and I moved up beside Alf. Then we went around peri track again. He said he was very happy and that we could proceed to do another circuit. So we went around the perimeter track once again. When we were back in dispersal he said we could have a short break. We clambered out of the aircraft and F/O Reeves said. 'I suggest you have a smoke if you like, and relax for ten minutes,' which we did.

When we were back in the aircraft, he stood behind me and said, 'Go ahead and start up.' I opened my window and yelled to the ground crew, 'Ready to start engines' and I pressed the starter button for the port outer and we proceeded to get all four started. When all engines were running smoothly F/O Reeves said, 'O.K. take us around the peri track and back here.' Alf took the four throttles and opened up the engines, then using the two outers to guide the aircraft, drove it around the peri track. The brakes were operated by Alf's feet, as they were incorporated in the rudder bar pedals.

When we arrived back, F/O Reeves asked Alf to vacate the pilot's seat and took over. He instructed everyone to don helmets and plug into the intercom system. Before anyone could say anything we were moving toward the runway and we heard him say, 'J Johnny to control. Taxiing out.' The control replied with the same words.

We stopped parallel to the runway at the end of the peri track ready to turn onto it. F/O Reeves called up the tower and said, 'J Johnny clear to runway.' The Control Tower answered, and the aircraft moved forward and turned onto the runway. F/O Reeves said 'Take off checks' and Alf (doing my job) said 'Fifteen degrees flap', and lowered the flaps with the lever on the consol. Then it was 'Clear for Takeoff', and the control

Tower answered back that it was all clear. We started rolling down the runway.

The next thing I knew we were airborne!

'Undercarriage up.' Alf lifted the lever on the consol and repeated 'Undercarriage up.' As we climbed, it was 'Flaps up' and Alf again obliged. We flew around the airfield and turned around to fly parallel to the runway. F/O Reeves said 'Downwind' to the ground control, and after receiving the same in reply, called out 'Flaps.' Alf lowered them fifteen degrees.

When we turned into the line of the runway, it was 'Full flaps' and Alf lowered the flaps. Then it was 'Undercarriage down' and Alf lowered the undercarriage. Then he called up base, 'Funnels' and we landed and taxied back to the dispersal.

'Well that's your first flight in a Lancaster,' F/O Reeves said with a smile. Then he climbed out of the seat and indicated for Alf to move into it. Then he motioned me to move up to my position. He then stood behind me and said to Alf, 'Take us around the airfield.'

Alf called up control and told them what we were doing and we proceeded to taxi all around the airfield. When we were opposite the dispersal F/O Reeves said to Alf, 'Now it's your turn, take us on a circuit of the airfield, and I mean in the air.'

Alf called up the tower and with their permission, started taxiing to the runway to take off for a circuit. We then taxied to the edge of the runway and Alf turned to me and said, 'When we start rolling, they are my throttles, and when I say 'Yours' you take them in exactly the same position up to the gate. Then line them up and take them through the gate to full power.'

It was only then that I realised that during taxi and take-off, when the aircraft is moving slowly, the only way to steer is with the engines and brakes. The two outer engines are used to keep the aircraft going in a straight line.

Although this aircraft is clearly on the ground, it shows the cramped space surrounding the Flight Engineer's panel. (Photograph with permission, Imperial War Museum. CH. 12469.)

We reached the end of the runway and turned on to it, and I applied 15 degrees of flaps. Alf said, 'Here we go' and we rolled down the runway, with Alf jiggling the throttles about but gradually moving them forward until he yelled 'Your throttles' and I took over. I moved them evenly to the gate and then through to full power.

As we left the ground Alf ordered, 'Undercart up' and I retracted the undercarriage. Then, 'Flaps up' and I raised the flaps with the lever, and we were climbing up into a blue cloudless sky.

By the time we had done several circuits and bumps, we were thoroughly enjoying life and performing quite efficiently. F/O Reeves informed us that we were clear to move on tomorrow to 'proper flying.'

The next day, with F/O Reeves behind me, we did 'circuits and bumps' in the morning and a short cross-country flight in the afternoon including banking searches. When searching the ground, the only one who can look down vertically is the bomb aimer, so if we all need to look, the aircraft is banked to left or right for greater visibility. Fortunately, this is a rare maneuver.

On our third day we did a practice bombing run on the bombing range in the morning. This was a large field in open country. In the afternoon we did another flight in which F/O Reeves showed us the actions to take if we were caught in a searchlight beam, and another practice bombing run on the return. We didn't actually drop anything, it was only our second day in the aircraft!

The next day we were on our own, without guidance or calming words from F/O Reeves. We flew a long cross-country: Base, Basingstoke, Bude, Worcester, Boston, Base, and between Boston and Base we practiced another bombing exercise. This was the first time we were in charge and Charlie, the bomb aimer, had to direct Alf with course changes at the appropriate time.

Alf had said that I should be able to fly the plane in an emergency and so the next day during our flight, he would let me have a go. The next day was exercise six, fighter affiliation. We had to fly a cross-country route for approximately four hours and during it we would be attacked twice by a fighter.

We took off an as instructed, climbed to 8,000 feet and set off on course. We had been going for about two hours when Charlie said, 'I thought this was a fighter affiliation trip.' It was hardly out of his mouth when there was a loud cry from Pete, 'Corkscrew Left' and Alf dived the plane to the left and quickly turned to the right, then climbed back to the left and then turned right. Alf did that twice while Pete was calling that the Spitfire attacking us was trying to follow us.

Then suddenly Pete called, 'All clear.' The maneuver is called 'Corkscrew' and is called with Left or Right added according to the direction of the fighter attacking. The Spitfire flew ahead, turned, and came back toward us doing a barrel roll in salute before heading off. We leveled off and continued on course. That was some experience for us novices.

On the return trip to base Alf engaged the autopilot, 'George,' and climbed out of his seat. He told me to take over and I climbed up into his seat. I disengaged 'George' and for the first time in my life I was flying a Lancaster!

I was nervous as Hell. It was very uncomfortable as Alf wore a full parachute, which fitted into a recess in the seat. When I sat in it I just sank into the space. I had a clip on type parachute that fitted on to the front of the harness I was wearing. I had to collect my 'chute' and put it in the well of the seat in order to sit comfortably.

Alf said, 'Relax, you can't fly like that.' He said, 'It really flies itself so it only needs a nudge now and then.' I tried to relax and was thrilled to bits to be flying the Lanc. After about ten minutes Alf took over again and we resumed our normal duties.

The next day we were told to report to the admin office instead of the briefing room. We rolled up at 9 a.m. and were met by a Flying Officer who asked if we were Alf Cowley and Co.? Alf said 'Yes.' The F/O said 'Follow me.' We walked around the H.Q. Buildings to a small hut at the rear. He pushed open the door and said, 'Come in.'

We followed him in to a room with what looked like a big circular tank about 10 feet long with a door in the end. It was unusual as it looked as if it was sealed all round. However, we were not in doubt long. A Flying Officer came up and said, 'This is an oxygen tank which simulates altitude. You will all get in and we will seal you in and then we will create an altitude of 20,000 feet. You will be wearing helmets with oxygen masks and we will give you pens and paper pads to write on. We want you to write down the names of your families, relations, friends and anyone you know, just keep on writing. Don't stop until you hear us tell you to do so.'

We all went in and sat facing each other on the two bench seats. Alf said we were to start writing, so I commenced writing the name of my relations, friends and anyone else I knew. Suddenly I was looking at a load of rubbish and squiggles on my paper, and we all started laughing at the same time. We had not realized that we were writing without control. We were told over the inter-com to come out, and when we lined up outside the F/O said, 'That gentlemen is what happens when you are starved of oxygen. This test is to make you careful to always have a clean and secure connection when at altitude.'

'We took you up to the equivalent of 20,000 and switched off your oxygen. You did not know and hence the lack of normal behavior.' He turned to me and said, 'It's primarily your job to see that the oxygen is flowing, and that the supply is maintained. Keep your eye on it.' This was a new job I had not encountered or been told about in training!

There were always things to do, even when we were not flying. One afternoon we sat around with red goggles on, in a small room without windows, the room was totally dark. After a period to let our eyes get accustomed to the dark, there would be a little flash of light somewhere on a wall, and we were supposed to identify the aircraft. It was so quick, I didn't even realise that the flashes were aircraft projected onto the walls as they were exposed only very briefly.

The gunners, however, had done it before in their gunnery training, and Pete was very good at recognizing the different aircraft. The second time we tried, I was a little better, but I was never very good at it. My aircraft recognition was excellent, but my seeing in the dark was not. Thank goodness we had Pete, but I was not impressed with the mid-upper gunner, Ian, who seemed no better than me.

We had been at Bottesford about five days when Alf came to the billet early in the morning. He called Ian out and they walked away. They were gone about fifteen minutes and Alf came back alone. He came into the billet and said that he had told Ian he was not up to scratch, and he was no longer a member of our crew. He said that we would be getting another mid-upper gunner in a day or two.

In fact it was only the next day when Alf turned up with a Flight Sergeant gunner, who he introduced as Norman Bolt. Norman had already done a tour of operations, 30 trips, and in my opinion had foolishly volunteered for another tour, his second, which would be another 20 trips.

Norman was from Yorkshire, in his late twenties, darkish, and with an accent that revealed his roots. He turned out to be a very nice man, and an extremely good gunner. This episode endorsed my view that Alf was a very nice chap but utterly ruthless when it came to the supervision of his crew and their duties.

After a week we moved on to night flights. At first, taxiing around the dispersal and the peri track in the dark was strange. The lighting around the dispersals was good but almost non-existent around the perimeter track, which was quite narrow. Everyone had to keep an eye out and warnings of wandering off track had to be prompt and clear, like 'Off to port!'

The first time we took off in the dark was unnerving. However, with practice we soon became acclimatized to night flying. I really enjoyed the long cross-country night flights. Somehow the world was a smaller place.

After four days of night exercises we were warned that we were to move on to longer night flying, and to rest in the afternoons. The next night we were scheduled for a long cross-country, and we were to be prepared for any eventuality.

It turned out to be a clear moonlit night; the reflection of the moon in the rivers was beautiful. As we flew along we were surprised by a fighter attack, which we had not been warned about!

It was a Spitfire, according to Norman, and he said that it was part of the training schedule for things like that to happen.

The crew in front of our favorite Lancaster, HA/U (Uncle). Standing from left to right Pete Green (Rear Gunner), me (Flight Engineer), Alf Cowley (Pilot), Charlie Lane (Navigator), Norman Bolt (Mid-Upper Gunner). In front: Mac McGair (Wireless Operator), Bob Davies (Bomb Aimer).

On aircraft specifically allocated to training only, the guns were fitted with cameras, which in the later stages of training, recorded the firing of the guns and filmed the effects. The fighter people then advised our superiors what the result was, i.e. would we have been shot down, or did we evade the attack, or was the fighter shot down.

At the end of two weeks each crew had an examination. First we flew with a Flight Lieutenant, who was a very experienced pilot, on a cross-country trip and had to perform various maneuvers when directed. We were suddenly attacked by a hurricane fighter, and then had to do a practice bombing run on the homeward section. I should explain that Fighter Command and Bomber Command cooperated in training flights for the mutual benefit of all crews.

Then we had a written exam, which the crew took in pairs, separately in different rooms. The gunners were paired off, as were the navigator and bomb aimer, and the pilot and engineer. The wireless operators were on their own.

The pilots and engineers were in a room with each pair sat at a trestle table. Questions were projected onto the far wall with separate questions for the pilots and for the engineers. We were given pens and paper and told to get on with it.

I thought the Flight Engineer's questions were very easy and finished quite quickly. I looked at Alf and to my surprise his paper was blank. He slid it across and whispered, 'This is your job. I fly the aeroplane.' To say I was shocked was the least of my feelings, but I took his paper and started writing. Fortunately, his questions were even easier than mine, so I finished it in time to pass it back before they were collected.

The following day we were assembled and the results of the practical exercises were read out, merely 'passed' or 'failed.' All the crews except two passed, and they were referred for additional training.

The results for the written tests were then read out. Alf scored 980 out of 1,000, while I scored 950. I was really annoyed, but Alf only laughed. We were the top crew, and the only crew graded as 'above average.' There were only three grades, above average, average, and below average.

Flying Officer Alf Cowley's Log Book Entries for our Bottesford training.

We were not told until we reached the Squadron that it was rare for a sprog crew to be graded as 'above average.' The following morning we were assembled and told what our postings were. We were posted to Bomber Command and we found that we were one of two crews posted to 218 Squadron at Chedburgh, which was near Bury St. Edmunds in Suffolk.

We were now to join Bomber Command, an organization of 93 airfields spread from Cambridge in the South to Darlington in the North. Operations varied in the number of aircraft flying, building up in numbers as the Lancasters came off the production line. The maximum number in any raid reached 1,000 bombers in 1945. Having this many aircraft going to one target needed careful organization and timing.

The entry from Alf's Log showing that we were "Above Average," a rare occurrence for a sprog crew.

It was obvious that the first aircraft would need to be leaving from the south so that succeeding squadrons would just join in at the rear. Collisions in the air were a complete disaster and to be avoided at all costs. The leaders of those squadrons would of necessity, be doing the navigation for the raid. Of course, every aircraft had a navigator, who had to know where they were every moment in case of problems maintaining their position in the formation. It also followed that the leaders of the raid would have to be the best crews.

Hence, when we 'sprogs' were assigned to Chedburgh, it was because we had been deemed fit for 218 Squadron.

We were given a weekend pass of 3 days and told to report to Chedburgh on return. Before we left Alf called us all together and said that he had been given our rating for the course. He was very pleased to report that we had been graded first of the group, and that our 'Above Average' rating was very rare amongst inexperienced crews. He said that we had earned our break and to go and enjoy it.

I spent the three days back home in Cardiff, walking around in the day, and dancing at night. It was good for my morale and very relaxing. It was Christmas time, but despite my mother's valiant efforts to make it special, my father ruined it. The only explanation was, it seemed to me, that he was jealous of my relative success.

At the end of my leave I caught a train from Cardiff to Paddington and crossed London to St. Pancras, and then caught a train to Bury St. Edmunds.

When I alighted from the train, I found myself among several airmen, ground staff and aircrew. One aircrew sergeant asked if I was one of the new crew for 218 Squadron? I said that I was and he said, 'Come with me, I'm stationed at Chedburgh.' We went out from the station into the car park where a 3-ton truck was waiting. He said, 'This is our taxi, climb aboard.' We climbed up into the back and were joined by several other airmen, both ground staff and aircrew.

When we arrived at the airfield, I found that Chedburgh was a 'war time aerodrome' the buildings being mainly Nissen huts, prefabricated buildings, and hangars. The aerodrome was a large oval shape surrounded by a wide road (the perimeter track) with roads feeding parking areas (dispersals) off outwards from the peri track.

There were dispersals at the northern end with Stirlings parked there. This was a separate squadron. 218 Squadron occupied the southern and western sides of the aerodrome. Each dispersal had 3 to 5 Lancasters parked on aprons (a circular area of concrete) and there seemed to be a large number spread around the area. Inside the peri track was a large triangle of three runways, with one longer and wider than the other two. This was the main runway and it was along the prevalent wind direction, so could be most commonly used.

CHAPTER 7

CHEDBURGH

I arrived at Chedburgh on the 15th January, 1945. I was 19 years old and despite over twelve months in the R.A.F., I was still lacking self-confidence. I had now all the qualifications for the job I had to do and despite having excellent marks all through, I didn't have the carefree air of so many of the other aircrew.

Also, my crew seemed different to the other crews, who were seven young men always together in the mess or town, or even the local pub. Apart from Bob and me, the others of our crew were all individuals, and there was no socializing between us. Alf was an officer and stayed in the officer's billet. I did not find out until after the war that Charlie was married and his wife was living in Bury St Edmunds. Hence, he sloped off at every opportunity. Pete was also married, and his wife was somewhere local living in rooms. This was the reason that we were not like the other crews in the mess. There were only the three of us around, Bob, Norman and me, and Norman was a loner, so Bob and I were the only ones of our crew in the mess at night. However, I have to say that if we were on a Battle Order, the six of us were there promptly at our pre-flight meal.

The village of Chedburgh was tiny and immediately opposite the camp gates was a house in which the ground floor had been converted into a shop. I later found that it sold just about everything we might require. An old-fashioned parlor had been converted to the shop with a doorway into the middle room, which was also part of the shop. The proprietor was a very friendly and elderly gentleman with old-fashioned manners.

I reported to the orderly room and was welcomed by a Warrant Officer who explained the geography of the site, pointing each thing out on a wall map. He showed me the billet we had been allocated, and said that each crew had its own billet. He explained about meal times and pointed out where the Sergeants' mess was. Finally, he said 'Carry on Sergeant Warburton, I'm sure we will see each other again soon.'

I picked up my kitbag and made my way to the billet, where I found Bob already settled in. It was the usual Nissen hut with a stove in the middle, but this time we had a coke scuttle. Bob said, 'We are lucky, we have a corporal in charge of our billet and he sees that it is cleaned and the coke bucket is full and on occasions when we are not around, to light it. He will see it's going on our return. Take your pick of the beds, mine's this one by the door.' I put my kitbag on the next bed to Bob's and opened up the adjacent locker. By now it was dinner-time, so we made our way to the mess and had a pleasant surprise. The mess was by R.A.F. standards, luxurious!

We went into the lounge and a Warrant Officer came over and introduced himself and welcomed us to the Squadron. 'I saw the look on your face when you came in and thought I'd fill you in.' He then explained that as the leading squadron, 218 had been adopted by the Gold Coast, a country on the west coast of Africa. He said they had been for some time, and still were, extremely generous, and provided all sorts of luxuries for us.

The lounge was very comfortable, and on the north wall was a large, beautifully furnished and well-stocked bar. The floor was carpeted, there were round tables with armchairs, and on the south wall were posh settees.

The bar prices were staggeringly low, less than half the price of the local pub!

The dining room next door was also well decorated and furnished with tables seating eight. The chairs were padded and upholstered. I had been sitting on metal chairs ever since I joined the Air Force, so this looked like the officer's mess to me.

On the right hand side of the dining room was a large table with a box of cutlery, on the right hand end adjacent to the cutlery was a pile of dinner plates. Further along was a shallow trough of large pans of different kinds of meat, most in deliciously smelling sauces. There was also a dish of fish cutlets, and dishes of vegetables.

Behind the table was an opening at table height, which led to a large, well furnished kitchen. The staff were all dressed like posh chefs with tall hats. One of them came forward and said, 'Welcome, I hope you have a safe and happy stay with us.' He said that we should take cutlery and a plate and help ourselves.

Beyond the food counter was a table with a tea urn and a coffee urn, as well as half-pint glasses with jugs of water. We took cutlery and a plate each and helped ourselves to a plate of food, and made our way over to the tables. Several of the tables were occupied and so we moved along to an empty one and sat down. Bob said, 'I think I'm going to like it here.' I agreed wholeheartedly.

After a desert we made our way out to the lounge and into the entrance hall with the Squadron Board on the right and a table below. This was just like

Bottesford, except that it was much more detailed and larger. Obviously, being a Squadron there were lots of aircraft flying in the same operation, whereas at Bottesford there were only single units. There was quite a bit of mail on the table, all laid out tidily in alphabetical order. The hall had a very nice carpeted floor in biscuit colour, adding an air of luxury.

Bob and I made our way back to the billet to find that the others had all arrived and settled in. They greeted us and we told them about the mess and our meal, which pleased them no end. We all agreed it had been a long day of traveling and that we needed an early night. We all agreed that it was not worth lighting the stove, so we did our toiletries in the wash-house that was just to the left of our front door. We had been told that we should report to the briefing room at 9 a.m. That was it, and we all retired.

The next morning Alf appeared at 8:30 a.m. at our billet and asked if we had enjoyed our leave. Each of us nodded and said that we had. Alf turned to me and asked if I would please come outside for a moment. We went out and he said that he had something to discuss with me.

Alf said that I was a first-class flight engineer, but that I was very immature and needed to grow up. "If I hear one more 'wizard' or 'jolly good show'" he said, "I will throw you out of the aircraft." He went on to say that we were fighting a war and it was not a picnic. "Grow up and be an airman."

At first, I was devastated and didn't know quite what to do. However, he took me by the shoulder and with a large grin on his face said 'Let's go and get on with the war.' We went back inside and he told the others it was time to go, and we all made our way to the briefing room.

The Briefing Room at Chedburgh was an improvement on Bottesford, but was in the same pattern. The three new crews (including us) were looking a bit apprehensive, except for Alf, who was his usual calm self. Each crew found a table and sat down. Promptly at 9 a.m. the Warrant Officer from the orderly room walked in with a Wing Commander, and introduced him as Wing Commander Smith, Officer commanding No. 218 (Gold Coast) Squadron. Wing Commander Smith moved to the front of the platform and said, 'My Squadron is the best in Bomber Command, and our standards are very high. We are frequently chosen to lead attacks on Germany, both by day and night. You new crews will have to work very hard to attain the necessary standards to become a part of this force.'

He went on to explain that we were equipped with Mark III Lancasters, and that we were part of No. 3 Group of Bomber Command, and that the squadron's history went back to the First World War. We had been chosen to be sponsored by the Gold Coast, an African country who provided us with additional facilities and luxuries, giving us more comfort than other stations.

He went on to say that there were three squadrons based at Chedburgh. First and foremost was 218. There was also a smaller Bomber Command Squadron flying Stirlings (4-engined bombers), and a small group belonging to Transport Command.

He then introduced the Squadron Administration Officer, who was a Flight Lieutenant. However, most admin officers didn't fly, and so I quickly learned from the others to call them 'penguins,' not in their ear-shot of course!

Anyone who didn't fly was called a penguin, and it could be used as derogatory slang for ground crew, but never for the maintenance boys. We needed them too much. The admin officer told us all we needed to know about existing at Chedburgh.

He was followed by Group Captain Brotherhood, who was a tall well-built man with a moustache, and very smart. He introduced himself saying he was the Station Commander and was responsible for everything on the aerodrome except the actual flying, which was our responsibility.

Compared to the distant and snobby Wingco, he was a really nice guy, who said that he was there to help us in any way he could, and we should never be afraid to call into his office in the main admin block near the Control Tower. In fact, we found that he was indeed a most helpful man. Throughout our time there, he looked after us exceptionally well on both service and private matters.

'Groupy' advised us that Chedburgh was a satellite drome of Stradishall, a peace-time airfield, which was the centre for two other satellite airfields as well as operating squadrons itself. He said that entertainment facilities were superior at Stradishall, where there was a cinema. When we were 'stood down' (stood down was the expression used for not being wanted or available for flying, such as injured, on leave, or given a few days off after a bad flight), we were welcome to go over to Stradishall to enjoy the facilities. It was about five miles away and there was a station crew bus every hour up to 11 p.m. and the driver was very nice to drunken aircrew.

Turning serious, he stressed that reporting time prior to an operation, was the crucial thing. If you were not at the briefing before the time stated, you would be in very serious trouble. He continued to say we were probably familiar with the squadron boards in the mess, but described it anyway. The lines listed the aircraft, pilot, and the names of the crew in each category. It was stressed that we should not just look at the pilot's name because if our pilot was not listed, we could individually still be listed with a different pilot, and would be expected to fly with another crew. This would happen if a member of a crew was injured or unable to fly for any reason.

We were told that unless we had been 'stood down', we must look at the orders every morning immediately after breakfast and in the evening after dinner. Some daylight flights left extremely early and so one needed to know the night before. There was also a crew listed without an aircraft. They were the reserve crew and must remain available in case a crew was unable to fly for some reason. Finally, the board listed the crews who would probably be on an operation the next day.

These crews were not to leave the station or have too much to drink! They were to be available at short notice and fit to fly. I guess the rumour had got around that aircrew drank a lot of beer.

The next morning, our first port of call was to the stores to draw our flying kit, which consisted of helmet, goggles, oxygen mask, and a whistle (in case we were shot down and landed in the sea, a whistle could be heard for miles, so they said!).

The oxygen mask also included a microphone, which was part of the aircraft inter-communication system and allowed everyone to communicate with one another. We had had to return our kit at Bottesford. However, here we would be issued with our kit to keep as long as we were with the squadron. Most was the same as we had at Bottesford, except that this was all new kit. We had quilted flying suits, one piece with long zips.

The gunners being in an unheated part of the aircraft had to have heated suits. They therefore had an additional outer suit, which was made from a very heavy material. These outer suits had electric elements for heating, as there was no heating aft of the main spar in the middle of the aircraft.

The cockpit was heated by air passed over the inner engine exhaust manifolds, and collected and distributed in the cockpit area. This was an effective form of heating, providing the engines were running and the pipes were not shot away.

Temperatures at 20,000 feet could be as much as 50 degrees below so one dare not touch the sides or any part of the airframe. If you touched the exposed metal with bare skin you were clamped firmly to it!

We also had three pairs of gloves, one silk, one wool, and one of large gauntlets. We were issued a pair of 'long drawers', old-fashioned long pants. Despite the jokes, we were assured that we would wear them and be very glad we did. We did and we were! We also had large white flying sweaters, the trade mark that everyone associated with aircrew, and which we wore with pride.

The next morning we 'sprogs' assembled in the briefing room and were given a series of lectures on being part of an operational station, our duties and responsibilities, and general information on what we were to know and do to be part of an efficient and effective squadron.

We also had a long talk followed by a question and answer session on being shot down and taken prisoner, and how to make efforts to escape capture. This was fascinating, as it was given by a chap who was shot down, escaped, and got back with the help of the French resistance. Undeterred, he was completing his tour.

He was a navigator on Lancs, and was shot down returning from a raid on Gelsenkirchen. He said that he managed to get out through the escape hatch in the bomb aimers compartment, and dropped by parachute into barren country. There was not a house or building for miles so he just walked what he thought was West, taking his time, looking for somewhere to hide. Some while later he came across a barn and hid in a loft under hay and slept until daylight.

He left the barn early and started to walk but was accosted by a farmer who turned out to be French. He didn't know it but he was over France when he bailed out. He was extremely fortunate that the farmer hid him and with his aid, the Underground Movement was contacted. Although it took a very long time, he was finally repatriated via Spain.

The last address was by Group Captain Brotherhood, the Station Commander, who summed up most of what we had been told and then said that the 'talking was over' and tomorrow would be the first day of our initiation into the Squadron. Fun was strictly for the mess, the rest of the time we were to be proud of the uniform we wore and act accordingly.

He said that we would also have a course on 'H2S' a navigational aid, and another on 'GEE,' a newer navigational aid. He emphasized that we had a great deal to learn before we would be ready for operations and needed to work hard. Finally, he said that each trade had their own section office and section leader, and we were to report there immediately.

We were then dismissed and told to report to No. 2 briefing room in the morning, which was used as the training briefing room for meetings. Even though we were still in training, orders would be posted exactly as raid briefing orders, and everything would follow the pattern of actual operations. We dispersed and each of us went to his section office.

I and the other flight engineers found the engineer's section and entered the office to find a Flying Officer with an engineer's brevet sat behind the desk. He stood up with a smile.

'Welcome to 218 Squadron. I hope you will be happy here and survive a full tour.' He showed us the logs that had to be filled in for every training flight or operation, recording the readings of petrol gauges every 30 minutes, and brief details of anything affecting the performance of the aircraft. He said that when flying, events happened so quickly that the log could easily be overlooked. He emphasized that the log was important in the diagnosis of faults, and was of great assistance to the ground staff on our return. Logs had to be handed in at the end of every flight. He said that he was always available and hoped we would keep him informed of our progress. He then wished us good luck, and we left.

The next morning we found that all the newcomer crews were listed for a 3 hour cross country flight, each with a training pilot. We were scheduled to have Warrant Officer (W/O) Veitch flying with us, and we were to report to the training briefing room. This chap had completed his first tour of 30 operations and after a spell of leave, was using his knowledge and experience to help us 'sprogs.'

As the bomb aimer, Bob's primary responsibility was to drop our bomb load on the target we were supposed to bomb. As this only took up a short period of time when we were at the target, he was trained in navigation and continuously helped Charlie do his job. So Bob attended the pre-briefing session for navigators, which took place before the full briefing of all crews, to learn the route to the target, and plot it on the copy of the map.

Charlie and Bob left us early after breakfast, to go to their pre-briefing, and when we got to the briefing room we found them sat at a table poring over maps and looking very busy. We joined them and sat down. On the front wall was a large map of Europe and across England was pinned a red tape showing our route around the bottom half of the country. From Chedburgh it went south to Southend, on to Brighton, right across to Bude, up to Stoke, then across to Norwich, and back to Chedburgh.

We had hardly time to breathe when a W/O called the roll and having found us all present, introduced two officers who were to brief us. They pointed out where we were going and what the turning points were. They said that take off times would be staggered with an hour's gap between the three aircraft. Then the weather report was read out, followed by the details of the flight: height to fly at, times of take off, etc.

When this was finished we were shown to the locker room where we donned our flying kit and made our way to the parachute store, where we each collected a parachute. Alf's had a harness which when donned made the parachute into a cushion; the rest of us had separate light harnesses around the shoulders and waist, and the parachute clipped on to the front when required.

We were the first crew out and so we went straight outside to the waiting bus and were taken out to our aircraft with W/O Veitch. He took Alf and me around on the aircraft checks with Chiefy, the flight sergeant in charge of all the ground crew for that flight. When satisfied he thanked Chiefy, and said we were to board the aircraft. We climbed in and I found that I had to stand behind W/O Veitch who was in my position.

As I passed Charlie's table I noticed a black box with a screen suspended on the rear of the wireless set and another adjacent to it. I asked what they were and was told that the first was the 'GEE' navigation aid, which operated over England and Wales but not over the other side of the channel. It needed ground stations and used a radar system to determine our position and sent the details to the set.

The other was H2S, the other navigation system. H2S used a scanner on the underside of the aircraft to show the silhouette of the ground below, showing the main geographical features. These were pieces of equipment fitted to the underside of the Lancaster.

After we had taken off and climbed to our cruising altitude of 10,000 feet and on course, W/O Veitch, who was now stood immediately behind me, suddenly said to me, 'Feather the port outer.' This meant that I switched off what is now called the ignition switch, to stop the engine, then turned the propeller blades in line with the slipstream so that the prop would not turn (feathering).

We were then flying on three engines. Alf was struggling to keep the aircraft from slewing due to the drag on the port side.

'You can trim that off, you know,' W/O Veitch said.

This meant that we could use the trimming tabs on the rudder to offset the feathered engine and compensate for the drag. Each control surface is fitted with a small replica of itself, which is controlled separately, enabling either the pilot or the engineer to set it to offset the main surface. This balances all the control surfaces, which makes the aircraft fly evenly. W/O Veitch stated that the Lanc was the only plane that could trim off the loss of an entire engine.

We flew on three engines for a while and then he said, 'Feather the port inner.' I repeated the process so that we were now flying on only two engines, and on one side. It was obviously a struggle for Alf but the plane flew on reasonably normally.

'There you are, you can fly this bird on two, but you cannot maintain height if there is any load. That is unique. It gives one great confidence to be flying on operations in an aircraft that is so reliable.'

'Start them up again', he said, and I restarted the engines and we returned to normal flying. Apart from being somewhat cramped in the cockpit area, the rest of the trip was a simple cross country flight and we seemed to be back at base in a short time. W/O Veitch was very complimentary after landing and said that we were cleared to join the squadron proper.

However, first we had to do yet another course. We had to learn how to use both the H2S and the GEE navigation systems, and each would require their own short course at Feltwell in South Norfolk. W/O Veitch said that we would fly to Feltwell, and stay for three days.

He went on to explain the procedure. 'The rest of you will be doing other exercises at the same time as they do their navigation course, such as fighter affiliation, in which you will be attacked without warning, and practice bombing on the way back.'

On January 24th 1945 one year after I joined the Air Force, we started our GEE and H2S courses. We had flown to Feltwell in HA/C and were billeted in wooden huts for a change. Bob and Charlie worked hard learning to use the new systems. They alternated positions to swap the use of the two units. Sometimes they were both buried behind Charlie's screen, and sometimes they were shouting to each other with Bob down in the nose.

We did long cross country flights both day and night and the rest of us had to do our jobs too. Finally on February 3rd at a briefing, before our flight, we were told we had to go to the briefing room the next day for our result. There we were told that we had passed the course.

'With flying colours!' Ha Ha.

The next morning we flew back to Chedburgh.

CHAPTER 8

OPERATIONAL

On our return to Chedburgh we were told that we were now approved for operational flying. This was the proudest moment of my life to date. Alf was beaming and congratulated us all saying we had done very well, and he was looking forward to us going into action together. We were all grinning like 'Cheshire Cats' and for the first time I felt that we were a united crew. I also, was suddenly confident in doing my job. Alf was no longer that remote and distant commander, he was still the captain, but he was also my friend.

We were told that Alf would be going as a second pilot on an operation before we undertook our first trip on our own. In fact, the next day Alf went off to Gelsenkirchen on a daylight raid with another crew and we stood around anxiously until he came back. We didn't see him properly until the next day when he came to the billet early in the morning.

Alf sat on Bob's bed and started to tell us of the operation. He said that it was not a comfortable flight for him as for most of the time he was stood behind the engineer. But he had a great view of the formation, they were number three on the right in the second 'Vic' from the very front of the formation.

The entire crew was on their second tour and it was the skipper's seventh trip, making it his 37th mission. Alf laughed and said we would have to buck our ideas up, as now he had seen how it should be done.

A few days later, there they were, our names on a battle order with a briefing time of 05:30 hrs. The aircraft was HA/G George, the target was Wesel, and the date was the next day, February 18th, 1944. We were called at 4 am the next morning and went for breakfast, the usual porridge, bacon, sausage and eggs, and toast.

To my surprise another fried egg was plonked on top. It was explained to us that when flying on an operation, we had a fried egg on top of whatever we were eating, irrespective of the time, or the menu. For night trips it was roast beef and gravy with an egg, or liver, bacon and gravy with an egg.

This was weird at first but we soon got used to it.

Charlie and Bob went to the main briefing room early for the route briefing and we followed on with the main group. We found our trestle table jammed in amongst so many that we could hardly walk between them, and took our seats. In front of the tables was a row of chairs and in front of that, a small stage against the wall. On the wall was a huge map of Europe and pinned to it was a long line of red ribbon, starting with a pin in Chedburgh and going due south across the channel and then south east across France, into Germany.

There were dog-legs here and there to avoid known German anti-aircraft sites. The ribbon proceeded, reaching the Ruhr Valley and Wesel and then coming back over France to England. A Flight Lieutenant was in charge and called the roll. Having established that everyone was present he sat down at the front.

Suddenly there was a cry of 'Attention.' We all stood up and several officers and a civilian came in. They sat in the front row and 'At ease' was yelled out. We relaxed and sat down. One of the officers, Wing Commander Smith, stood up and addressed the meeting.

Very soon we would come to call him 'Smithy,' our slightly disrespectful name for the Wing Commander. We overheard him referred to as 'Penguin Smith' by some crews, but it was only later on that we found this to be disrespectful because he would not fly at night.

When we queried this we were told that some time before he had put his name at the head of the crews to go on a daylight mission. Due to weather problems the operation was postponed and made into a night trip. Smithy is reputed to have crossed his name out. Hence it was rumored that he would not fly at night. I do not know if this was true but I do know that he did not fly at night whilst we were there.

Alongside Smithy on the platform was Group Captain Brotherhood, the Station Commander. His reputation was sky-high, and it was said that he would fly on every operation if he was allowed. We were told that he would do anything for any aircrew chap who needed help.

All officers who were actively flying were highly respected because, with the exception of Alf, they were all on their second tour. I have to admit that I only learned all this after I had been on the Squadron for some time and it gradually came out in bits and pieces.

Smithy welcomed the new crews and said that he hoped we would have a successful tour of operations. 'Gentlemen, today your target is Wesel, an important manufacturing area in the Ruhr.' He said that it would be a 5-hour trip, approximately. He told of the sites of factories, north of the towns, which were to be attacked, told of our bomb load, and that master bombers would be at a low level providing flares to mark our target. We were to bomb from 19,000 feet.

'For the new crews,' he said, 'I should explain that the master bomber is at low level to keep observation of the target area throughout the raid to ensure a distribution of bombing over the complete target.' He said that we would get instructions like, 'Bomb on green flares' or red, which would move the target around the area.

We were to be part of a raid consisting of over 500 bombers and our squadron was the leader. He said that the leader was identifiable by the broad white stripes on the fins and rudders. We were to take off at 11.00 a.m., and would assemble into formation whilst climbing on track. He advised which aircraft would be the main leader, the reserve leader, and that all the other aircraft should form an orderly formation in 'Vics' of threes. A 'Vic' is slang for three aircraft in a group, a leader and one aircraft positioned either side, and slightly behind. The stream then builds up by Vics forming on Vics.

'Be patient,' he said 'in forming up, a collision with full bomb loads would be a major disaster. New crews should take particular care.' The position of your aircraft in the whole armada was not defined; you formed or joined on, as you arrived, so that aircraft were not queuing to form up.

The next guy to stand up was the intelligence officer, a penguin Flight Lieutenant (another non-flying officer) who pointed out the parts of the route where flak might be expected and where the fighter aerodromes were. He said that we should stick to the way back shown, as far as possible, and to note that there was a lot of flak to the north of this track.

Then the civilian stood up and he turned out to be the 'Met' man, who told us what the weather was expected to be like, wind speeds at different altitudes, that the cloud would be at approximately 10,000 feet, and that it would be very patchy. He said that it should be clear in the target area.

Then Group Captain Brotherhood stood up and proceeded for the benefit of new crews to talk of the history of 218 (Gold Coast) Squadron, and how we very often led the attacks. He particularly and warmly welcomed the new crews and wished us well.

We later found that he was the opposite of Smithy as he had already done two tours and was always trying to fly on raids as a passenger, if he could. A first tour consisted of 30 operations completed successfully. That is, you got to the target and dropped your bombs, aborted trips did not count.

A second tour would be another 20 operations, but the number of airmen who completed a second tour was small. It is on record that over 8,000 bombers were shot down and that 55,000 airmen of Bomber Command were lost.

We dispersed and broke up with the bomb aimers and navigators staying in the room. Those of us engineers on our first trip were directed to No. 2 briefing room where we were addressed by the engineering leader, a Flight Lieutenant who had completed two tours. He told us what our total fuel load would be, what the bomb load consisted of, and issued us with logs, which we would have to fill in during the trip.

The log was a printed sheet with columns on the left for figures to be inserted. We were required to enter the fuel gauge readings every 30 minutes and also enter details of throttle settings. From this we calculated the theoretical fuel consumption, which was checked against the gauge readings. He stressed that the log took second place to our main duties.

He then told us about the device used on night flights for confusing the German radar. Aluminium foil strips were tied up into bundles, which were dropped out through a 'chute.' The top of the chute was on the engineer's side just under the front of his window. He said that the navigator would tell us when to start and finish. This was all on our sheet and we would find the bundles of strips in the nose compartment. It was our job to push these bundles down the chute one at a time.

The engineering leader explained that there was one other vital job for us. When the aircraft was on its bombing run we were to go down into the bomb aimer's compartment and open the small access plate on the front panel of the bomb bay.

As the bomb aimer called 'Bombs gone' we were to watch the bombs drop from the aircraft to ensure that all of them actually went. He reminded us that there were manual releases on all the bomb retainers and they were accessed from above in the fuselage floor. Each plate had two screws.

He reminded us that we had been shown the manual releases in case there were any bombs hung up. The news that bombs sometimes might not drop was not a happy thought, particularly since any stuck bombs were my problem!

At the bottom of the log was a space for us to report on our return, the performance of the engines and to note any damage or problems experienced. It suddenly struck me that at no time in our training had we been told of these log sheets. However they were elementary really, so it did not matter.

We were also expected to diagnose causes of problems to minimize time for the ground crew on our return. He said there were times when we would be 'rather busy' (an understatement!), but that we must always be aware of the fuel position. He pointed out that as there were a lot of planes on the same course and at the same altitude, we must keep our eyes open about what was going on around us. With that, he wished us good luck and we dispersed back to the briefing room.

We collected our flask of tea and packet of sandwiches, our sustenance for the 5 hours, and went to meet up with the rest of the crew at the locker room.

We changed into flying kit and put away everything we were not allowed to take with us. The only permissible thing to be carried was our 'dog tags,' plastic identity discs strung around our necks, indented with our name, rank and number, and a handkerchief. The whistle, which was supposedly used to attract attention should we be unfortunate enough to land up in the Channel, went on to the collar button so that it would be in the right place if we should need it.

We went to the parachute store where we collected our 'chutes' and learnt the old and oft repeated joke:

'If it doesn't open you can have your money back!'

We sprogs were yet again lectured on the fitting of the chutes. Operating the clip-on type chute was supposed to be simple: Pull the handle on the right hand side.

But even as a young, immature flight engineer, I could see that it was a bad design. The handle was fitted on one side of the chute, so it could be mistakenly clipped on with the handle on the left. Stories were told of bodies being found on the ground with an unopened chute still clipped on, but with a hole caused by frantic scraping to find the handle, which was on the other side. This design was good for moving around the aircraft, since space was so limited, but not so good when you had to bail out in a hurry. We were advised that as we were always at dispersal with time to spare, new crews should spend some time putting the chute on and off.

We went outside and waited for transport out to the dispersals. If you were lucky, you had a crew bus, but mostly it was 3-ton lorries and you just jumped up into the back. The lorries toured around the aerodrome dropping crews off as they went, until we reached 'G George' and off we got.

Alf and I were greeted by Chiefy. I toured the aircraft with him inspecting all the control surfaces to ensure that the locking devices had been removed, and all the rest that was required of me. I had been advised never to imply that we did not trust the ground crew.

I looked up into the bomb bay and there smack in the middle was a 'cookie', a very large tin can which contained 4,000 lbs of high explosive, and 2 pairs of 250lb bombs in front and another two pairs behind.

'Everything's fine', I said, nervously. Chiefy said with a friendly smile, 'You did fine, all the right checks in the right places.' I was very relieved and smiled back and said 'Thank you for all your help.'

He said, 'It's O.K. You'll be fine from now on.'

We learnt now that additional time was always allowed at each stage so that take off time was maintained. We stood around chatting and smoking until Alf said it was time to go. We donned our parachute harnesses and 'Mae Wests,' the inflatable life jackets. Boarding an aircraft had to be done in the correct order, as it was difficult to pass each other in the narrow fuselage, particularly now with parachutes and Mae Wests.

The bomb aimer went first into the nose, then Alf. I followed him, then Charlie the navigator, Mac the wireless op, Norman the mid-upper gunner, and finally Pete the rear gunner. We took up our positions and did our pre-flight checks, and when all were completed I called out 'Start engines' to the ground crew.

I started all four Merlins, ran them up and checked the magnetos. I closed the bomb doors and we were ready to roll. I signaled to the ground crew to disengage the accumulator trolley, used to start the engines, so saving the aircraft's internal batteries.

Alf called to each member of the crew in turn to check that the intercom was working OK. I signaled to the ground crew to remove the chocks from the wheels. We commenced taxiing and made our way out onto the perimeter track where we joined a long line of Lancasters making their way around to the main runway and taking off in turn.

No communication to the control tower by radio was allowed, only the intercom within the aircraft. It was stressed that 'Gerry' could pick up radio communications, which would alert them. So no radio communication was allowed between aircraft or with the control tower. We merely followed the Lanc in front until we turned onto the runway and it was our turn.

At the start of the runway there was a caravan and inside in a blister top was a guy with an Aldis signaling lamp to give us the 'Go' by a green light. What surprised us was that there was quite a crowd around the caravan, airmen and WAAFs of all ranks, waving and showing the thumbs up sign.

Finally we got a green and roared off down the runway with Alf jockeying the four throttle levers with his right hand and using his left hand on the control column.

We called this 'The last cigarette.' With everything ready to go, we hung around smoking, waiting for start up of engines. Left to right: Alf, Mac, Charlie, me, Bob, Pete, and Norman. Pete and Norman are in their heavy, electrically heated gunner's suits.

This was our first time with a full load of bombs and the speed and acceleration was noticeably different. I began to wonder if we would be airborne before the end of the runway, stupid really when it was happening every day.

We picked up speed and the tail came up and suddenly. Alf said 'Your throttles', so I slowly moved the throttles forward in the same positions. They were staggered quite a lot but I leveled them as I pushed them through the gate for full power. At last we lifted off and Alf said, 'Gear up' and away we went with sighs of relief all round.

With all those bombs, climbing was noticeably slower than we had grown accustomed to in a light aircraft. We climbed up following the other aircraft on course, and jockeyed around until we found a position in the formation. Although there had been dire warnings about this procedure, we found that as every Lanc was flying the same course it was O.K., so long as you did not jump the queue. Alf calmly sought out our position and we tucked nicely in to the right and slightly behind another Lanc. We continued climbing, heading toward France, and watched the main formation closing up without any bother.

We realised that being in the early part of the formation was a tremendous advantage because it gave us forward visibility. We flew along with other squadrons joining on behind, climbing all the time until we were at 19,000 feet and aircraft stretched behind as far as we could see.

Aircraft formed into Vics of three. A Vic is three aircraft with a leader and one each side formated just behind the leader. Two Vics fall in behind the leading Vic, and the formation builds up gradually to a width of twelve aircraft and so the line of aircraft build up behind. We were in the rear of the first group of twelve aircraft, which meant we were slightly lower than them and so we had good visibility of where we were going. We saw the coast of Southern England.

Bob called to Charlie exactly as we passed over the English coast giving him an exact fix of our position. This was essential for Charlie, for not only did it give him our position but it told him the effect of the wind. I should explain that the wind has a precise effect on an aircraft. If the wind is blowing at say twenty miles an hour against the course the aircraft is following, the aircraft will move forward twenty miles an hour slower.

Then we crossed the channel and the French coast came into sight. In a very short time we crossed into enemy territory for the first time. We had not gone far into France when small black puffs appeared all around us and it suddenly dawned on me that that this was flak, as we called anti-aircraft fire.

The engines made so much noise that one could hear no other noise except for the talk on the intercom, which was always kept to a minimum, and the 'puffs' seemed harmless. A little later on we learnt just how 'harmless' the puffs were when a Lancaster further down the formation just exploded into a ball of yellow, red and black smoke and fell towards the earth. The German guns were usually in batteries and fired simultaneously so that they created a box of exploding shells. Anything in the box was badly damaged and usually shot down.

The damaged aircraft did not catch fire, but seemed to lose control, which was probably due to the shrapnel hitting a vital part. It dropped one wing and spiraled down toward the earth and we lost sight of it.

Fortunately, we did not see any more losses and we proceeded to the target without too much trouble. Whenever we crossed a coast, or if there was some large landmark or river, Bob would tell Charlie so he had a fix, an exact point of our position.

As we approached the target we heard the master bomber over the intercom, saying, 'Bomb on red.' We looked down and spotted a Lancaster at low level flying above what appeared to be a lot of factories. There were one or two flares close to the ground and Bob said 'Target in sight.' Suddenly red flares exploded over the factories and Bob, now in charge of the aircraft as the bomb aimer, started to direct Alf, who had widened the gap slightly from the other aircraft. Suddenly, Bob said, 'Bomb doors open.' I opened the bomb doors, while Bob continued to direct Alf from his position prone in the nose compartment, eyes glued to the bomb site.

I then descended into the nose, pressed against the bulkhead, and opened the small trap door, looking back into the bomb bay. Bob was guiding Alf, 'Steady, steady, right, steady ...' Then there was a short pause and a loud, 'Bombs gone.'

When Bob said that, it was my job to see that all the bombs left as intended, and that none had hung up, still nestling in our bomb bay. The 500-pounders went first, and in sequence: first one from the back, and then one from the front. They also varied from side to side so the aircraft remained steady. After the last 500-pounder dropped, there was slight pause before the cookie dropped.

One press by Bob released all the bombs, but it would not be funny if a 500-pounder dropped on top of the cookie. So there was a gap between the 500-pounders going and before the cookie left. The order was essential as the cookie descended slower than the other bombs, and if the cookie went first, the smaller bombs could hit it on the way down.

I said 'All gone', closed the trap door and scrambled back to my position, where I closed the bomb bay doors. Immediately, Alf dropped the nose and turned away to get out of the traffic and head for home. We had been told that planes did not necessarily reform to return home, so we merely put our nose down and got out of there sharpish.

Alf and I had discussed the options, which were to dive like mad to a relatively low level to get maximum speed to get away from the target area, or to do a slower descent over a longer period.

Pythagoras came into his own, and I convinced Alf that we should use the hypotenuse of the triangle to our advantage. We would benefit as our fuel consumption would decrease by descending more slowly over a longer period and at a slightly slower speed. Lots of aircraft took a different approach and formed up on the return, obviously believing that the concentrated defense of lots of guns was safer.

Once well away from the target area we relaxed and I was back to my normal duties of keeping the propellers synchronized so that the engines ran smoothly, keeping track of the fuel, and transferring it from the wing tanks to the main.

It was soon apparent that the Germans were now alert to the target and therefore knew the direction of our return. Gerry had ack-ack guns mounted on trains and these were used to effect on returning aircraft. This meant that sometimes the flak was much heavier on return journeys.

We witnessed one aircraft being hit and suddenly woke up to the fact that this was not a picnic and our excitement that we had done our job turned to concern. We weren't home yet. It had seemed a long trip out, but it seemed an even longer trip back to the Channel coast. Eventually there it was, and then there was Chedburgh. We landed safely, taxied to the dispersal, parked the aircraft, shut everything down, and finally relaxed.

We climbed out of the aircraft and were met by the ground crew who gave us cigarettes and asked about the trip. I found Chiefy and reported on the aircraft's performance, and that it had been a very good flight with no damage to the aircraft.

We were picked up by the trucks and taken to the debriefing room, where there was tea and coffee. There were several tables at which two men sat. We waited our turn and then went to a vacant table where two gentlemen, who turned out to be intelligence officers were waiting.

We all sat around and the questioning started. It was a polite third degree. Where was the flak? Did we see any fighters? Did we see anyone go down? Where and when? Was the target clear? Finally, they were satisfied and told us to carry on. These gentlemen, on completion of the debriefing, entered into records the information we provided.

These were the Operational Record Books that Margaret found in the National Records Office at Kew, which have enhanced the accuracy in this tale.

We were all tired and made for the billet, where an early night was called for. It was a very long day, it seemed a lot longer than the stated 'five hours.' What we soon realized was that the 'five hours' was only the flying time. With the briefing and all that went on before and the debriefing after, it was a very long day.

The very next day we were listed for an op, another daylight run with briefing again at 05:30. This time we were in 'Q Queenie,' and we were off to Wesel again.

For the first two hours or so, it was a calm and peaceful flight. Suddenly the aircraft, two away on our starboard side erupted into a huge flaming mass and fell away, and we were showered with shrapnel. Holes appeared in our fuselage, but fortunately no one had more than a scratch.

It was one of ours, 218 Squadron, and we had to record the time and place. It was part of Charlie's duties to record these sorts of things. We kept looking for parachutes but saw none. We flew on and the aircraft was soon out of sight, but it was a very frightening episode. On our return we found we had lost a very experienced crew, which showed that it was all a game of chance.

After the debriefing we went straight to our billet, tired out. I was lying in my bed that night unable to sleep and it suddenly dawned on me that Bob and I were alone in the billet. The others all disappeared immediately they had showered and changed. I mentioned earlier about Charlie and Pete being married but at that time we, that is Bob and I, did not know, so their disappearances were a mystery.

Two days later we were on the battle order for Dortmund, our first night operation. It rained all day and when we went to briefing we were all damp and cold. Our waterproof capes kept the rain off but the atmosphere made our clothes damp. We had dinner at 5:00 p.m. and it was a really good roast, but somehow having a fried egg on top of meat and gravy did not seem quite right.

The briefing at 6:00 p.m. was packed, and it was what was described as a 'maximum effort,' every available aircraft was used. The map showed up my poor geography for I thought we were in for a long trip but in fact it was only just out of the Ruhr. We went to dispersal to 'V Victor' and found it to be quite an old Lancaster with a lot of bombs painted on the front side. Underneath the pilot's window on the side of the aircraft, the ground crew painted a bomb for each operation flown by the aircraft. 'V Victor' had quite a history.

'You've got a lucky one tonight, good for you,' Chiefy said. We climbed aboard and did all the checks and started up. When Alf was happy, we taxied out joining into a long stream. Taxiing in the dark and rain was not a pleasant start, and being damp did not help. However when it came to our turn, we took off and climbed on course joining the other aircraft, who whilst not in tight formation, just flew along together. Formation is impossible at night and very dangerous. There were no lights on the aircraft, and even Charlie's little light over his table was shielded by a complete floor-to-cabin roof curtain.

We flew on into Germany when suddenly we were picked up by a searchlight. The cockpit was brighter than day and we were totally exposed. It was frightening. Alf tried diving and then quickly pulling up but was restricted by the fear of colliding with the other aircraft. Alf suddenly put the nose down and did a diving turn and fortunately the beam lost us. That was probably the most frightening moment of my tour to date. We were totally exposed and the flak became intense. When we got to the target there were not a lot of fires around the target. However, the flares were clear.

We were told over the intercom by the master bomber who was circling the target at low level, to 'Bomb on red.' I looked down and saw red flares exploding over the target and Bob said, 'Got them' and directed Alf, and suddenly it was 'Bombs gone.' I was down with Bob looking through the hatch and watched them all go, and confirmed so to Alf. He said, 'Right, let's go home' and the aircraft banked and turned sharply around and we immediately started descending.

We had an uneventful flight home and landed without a problem, as we were one of the early arrivals. Although it was only a five and a quarter hour trip, it was tiring, and so it was a quick wash and bed.

The next morning we were told that we had three day's rest. One of the 218 (Gold Coast) Squadron crews had finished their tour and there was to be a big party in the sergeants' mess. A tour was thirty ops and we thought that it was quite an achievement. The officers had been invited into our mess too, so it was a Squadron party.

Not knowing the routine we were early and W/O Veitch was there and greeted us warmly. He said that as we hadn't been to a do like this before he would 'wise us up.' He said that firstly the drinks were free, part of the Gold Coast support. After a few drinks we would have a special dinner, and very unusually, there would be drinks with dinner.

He said that some time after the meal there would be a contest. Crews would play a sort of game, five at a time. The furniture would be removed from the long wall and the five crews would space themselves along it.

Then two members would bend down from the waist, the first leaning on the wall. It was called 'Reliego' (pronounced rel-ee-ay-go).

The second chap would lean on the first forming a long back. Then the other members of the crew would have to take a running jump to land and stay on the other two. The object was for all the rest of the crew to have their legs off the floor for ten seconds. The successful crews would then carry on until there was a winner. By this time the mess was full and someone said that dinner was served. We all trooped into the dining room and had a lovely dinner served by WAAFs.

The drink flowed, the room was very noisy, and there was a lot of laughter. It was a great atmosphere. Immediately the last plate was removed, W/O Veitch stood up, 'Right you lot, before you get too pissed, let's get on with it.'

It seemed that the majority had done this before and there was a mass withdrawal into the lounge. Crews were given numbers and the first five were called. What followed was the most hilarious, rough house I have ever been a part of. Being the complete novices, we were soon out, but the old hands were very good and it was amusing, rough and damn good fun.

Each member of the crew that won was given a bottle of beer, and they all thought it was great. For me, it was a unique evening and an education. I had never experienced anything like it before.

Two days later we were in the mess looking at the battle order and noted that we were not wanted, as Alf's name was not there. Bob pointed out that my name was and I was to fly with F/Lt. McKenzie the following day, and that we were going to Gelsenkirchen. It was McKenzie's second tour and all of his crew except for one of the gunners, were also on their second tour. His flight engineer had been taken ill and I was the replacement.

I was very apprehensive, particularly at briefing when I met the crew. McKenzie was the superior type, and did nothing to make me feel comfortable. Fortunately, it turned out to be a very good flight with no problems. After debriefing he turned to me and said, 'Well done. I was apprehensive about a very young sprog but you performed well.'

I was extremely pleased and flattered. My duties were to manage the throttles, operate the flaps, lift and lower the undercarriage, and keep the engines synchronized. The latter was necessary because if the engines were not synchronized there was an uncomfortable vibration through the frame of the aircraft. In daylight one looked through the inner propeller at the outer and adjusted the pitch of the blades until the hazy sight of the propellers looked like they were turning. When synchronized they looked as if they were stationary. At night one had to do it by sound. To receive an accolade from such an experienced and high-ranking officer was indeed a compliment.

Several aircraft were lost but none from our squadron. We were always told at the end of breakfast the following day, how well the previous day or night's operation had gone and if there were any losses.

These figures came from the B.B.C. news which merely gave the fact that the raid had taken place, on which town, and how many aircraft had been lost on the whole operation by all squadrons. Our sense of losses was from the people in the mess. If the mess was full, new crews had arrived, if it was nearly empty, we had had a bad day or night.

A portion of Alf's Log, recording our first few operational missions.

Looking back it only now strikes me how few friends we made, apart from our own crew. It was like living in an ever-changing population. Losses, completion of tours and leave meant that the only constants were our own crew. In the debriefing hall after an 'op' there were up to ten crews being questioned and one looked around and if we knew them, they and we would exchange smiles and 'thumbs up.'

Alf occasionally let me fly the aircraft. As Alf put it, it was part of my job in an emergency. This was the best part of my life in the R.A.F. To sit in the pilot's seat with complete control over a Lancaster and actually be flying it with the encouragement of Alf was something special. Actually it was easier than I thought, it actually flies itself, you only have to do things to change course or climb or dive.

Our fifth operation was a daylight trip to Lommersum, a five-hour operation, so they said, and all went as planned initially. We were approaching the German border and I was looking out of my side window when the rear gunner, Pete, yelled 'Corkscrew starboard.' I looked up and back to the right and there, coming down from a reasonably high point was a Focke-Wulf fighter.

I was mesmerized as he dived toward us with the tracers from his canon shells coming straight down and into the starboard outer engine. The engine suddenly burst into flames and I yelled, 'Fire in the starboard outer.' I immediately pressed the fire extinguisher button.

Nothing happened!

The F.W. 190, for that's what it was, seemed to be right alongside for a moment and I could clearly see the helmeted head of the pilot. In a flash he was gone.

The engine continued to belch smoke and flames. I tried the extinguisher again, but knowing it only worked once, I knew it was not going to work. I told Alf to dive down to starboard, hoping the extra air pressure would put out the fire. We were down to 5,000 feet when suddenly the smoke stopped and the fire was out.

I called to Alf, 'Fire's out,' and he immediately pulled out and leveled off. We were now flying with a full bomb load at 5,000 feet and on three engines. We could not maintain our altitude, and Alf said we had to jettison our bombs. Charlie said that we were just about in Germany, so why not just jettison them.

I thought that a waste and said, 'How about we find a railway line on a northern heading, on our way home, and drop them on that.' We all agreed and proceeded on a northerly heading and fortunately quite quickly found a railway line. We followed it for about five minutes and Bob said, 'There's a factory down there, just ahead.' I looked down and thought it would have been more appropriate to say it was a garage, but under the circumstances we all agreed, and down went the full load.

Alf was now able to maintain height on three engines, and we continued on our way home, fortunately without further problems. As we approached Chedburgh Alf called in, 'Beanie Mike to base.' There was a roar from the tower.

'Welcome Back! We thought we'd lost you!' came over the headphones. Alf told them that we were on three engines and the tower said to come straight in. Alf asked what I thought of a three-engined landing. I suggested that as we had successfully trimmed off the lack of the fourth engine, we could go straight in, and that as soon as we were down, we should shut down the starboard outer and taxi on the inner engines only. Alf agreed and that's what we did.

When we got to the dispersal we were surrounded by ground crew all cheering and shouting. It was reported that we had gone down in flames. We climbed out of the aircraft and almost collapsed.

We were all exhausted. I don't know why, perhaps it was from stress, we certainly hadn't done any strenuous exercise. It had been a very nervous and frightening experience.

The Operational Record Book page from The National Archives. The mission to Lommersum on 23 February, 1945. With Permission. A transcript appears on the next page.

> Bomb Load. 1x4000lb HC., and 12x500lb. AN. .64 TD..025.
>
> Bombed on Gee fix last resort owing to inability to keep up with stream and climb as port outer engine was u/s.
>
> Rear Gunner saw bursts across village and bombs may have fallen across road and railway East of Lommersum, as they were set on distributor setting .35. We made certain we were in Germany before bombing by taking Gee fix and were attempting to bomb railway lines or marshalling Yards there.
>
> Diverted on return.

A transcript of the Operations Record Book account of our mission to Lommersum. There is no mention of the fighter attack, just that the port outer engine was u/s!

A crew bus arrived and out came Group Captain Brotherhood. He grabbed Alf's hand and said, 'Well done!' He turned to us and said, 'And to all of you, a splendid effort, getting home on three engines. Everyone said you had gone down in flames, and we had written you off.'

We climbed into the bus and went to the debriefing room where we were greeted again with the fact that we had been reported as gone down in flames, and lost. We were given cups of coffee, and found them laced with brandy. Alf said he thought it was worth it. Then we sat down with two interrogation officers and went through our operation in detail. As soon as they could, they wrapped it up, and we were sent off to our billets.

Three days later we received a message saying that our crew was to report to Wing Commander Smith's office. Alf came around and escorted us to the admin block and we were immediately ushered into the Wingco's office. He stood up, came around the desk and shook our hands. He called for extra chairs and we sat in front of his desk, while he retired back behind the desk to face us.

Smithy said that a Mosquito was sent out after every raid to check the route for jettisoning of bombs. He claimed that some crews would jettison their bombs before the target and turn for home. We did not believe this, and we certainly had not ever seen it happen. He said that the Mosquito had identified our target and that we had destroyed a substantial factory.

So much for the garage I thought we had bombed!

Smithy was singing our praise and said that the crew had been awarded a D.F.C.!

We naturally assumed that Alf would receive the D.F.C., but we found out later that he refused it, and insisted that it be given to our mid-upper gunner, Norman, as he was on his second tour. With Smithy's praises singing in our ears, we adjourned to the mess, got Alf the officer admitted, and had a huge celebratory party.

We had three days rest and then it was off again. This time it was to Gelsenkirchen, and it was pouring with rain. We taxied out from the dispersal, going cautiously along the perimeter track when suddenly we veered to the left and the aircraft left the track and swerved onto the grass. The left wheel sank into the mud, the aircraft slewed around, and finished up off the peri-track altogether.

There were people around us immediately waving and shouting and Alf opened his window as an officer yelled, 'Get the hell out of there sharp. Leave everything and run across to the dispersal and take the reserve aircraft.' He said, 'By the time you get there the engines will be running, so get off as quickly as possible.' We all donned our capes, left the aircraft, and ran down the perimeter track avoiding the following aircraft.

When we got back to the dispersal there was an aircraft with its engines running and ground crew waving frantically to us. We all piled in, took over control, and headed for the runway. This was the first time I was actually aware that there was always a spare aircraft loaded with bombs and fuel, ready to go in case of emergencies.

As we got to the peri track I noticed the aircraft were all going the other way around to avoid our foul up, so we followed them the wrong way around.

I realized that Alf was having difficulty seeing because the windscreen wipers were not doing their job. So I opened my window and stuck my head out to see where we were going. I yelled instructions to help guide him. We made it to the runway and took off.

We had been sent on a different route to Germany and encountered a lot of flak and were twice attacked by fighters. Fortunately for us they were concentrating on the large group behind us. Several aircraft were shot down but it all happened very quickly and the fighters disappeared.

We went to the target without further incident and as we approached the target there were fires over a large area, and I could see the bombs exploding around the flares. The master bomber told us to bomb on the green flares, which were a little off the main conflagration. Alf said he thought that was because they had bombed the wrong area at first.

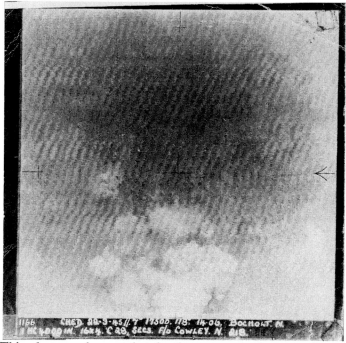

This photograph was taken by the camera in the nose of our aircraft, which was timed to delay the exposure until the bombs exploded. The white clouds at the bottom are the explosions of our bombs. This photograph was on the wall of the mess for several days as an example of successful targeting--until I took it down and kept it.

We had an uneventful trip home which was just pleasurable flying. Perhaps it is hard to understand this, normal flying as pleasurable, when just an hour earlier there were fighters shooting at us, planes exploding, bombs being dropped and exploding. There was a large feeling of relief when we turned away having dropped our bombs.

The feeling was possibly that we'd done what we came for, now let's go home, but certainly having done it, there was a definite relaxation in the atmosphere.

The next day we were off to Gelsenkirchen again on a daylight op, which was a breeze. We went all the way there and back and apart from a little flak here and there, we had no problems.

We had two days off and the following day we were off to Cologne, a five and a half hour trip with a lot more flak both there and back. We had some holes in the bottom and side of the fuselage but no one was hurt.

What really struck me was the completely flat area of flattened housing approaching the city and the cathedral standing out alone. There was nothing else near it. The city certainly had been destroyed, emphasizing the bombing damage. I felt guilty that firstly, here we were again, and secondly, I had helped to do this. At 20,000 feet dropping our bombs and turning away quickly had meant not witnessing what destruction we had caused, so no conscience.

On the 3rd March at short notice we were sent off on a special H2S training trip. Bob and Charlie were on a special course for a new system of navigation. Alf and I flew the aircraft to their instructions, but the gunners had a nice easy day enjoying the flying, as they did on all these courses.

The following day we were off to Wanne-Eichel again. As it was such a small town I wondered why, but we were later told that there were a considerable number of factories in the outskirts. We were at 19,000 feet and as we crossed into Germany we hit cloud, it was a dense layer, and we were led to a lower altitude by the leader.

We were down to 14,000 before it was completely clear and we ran into some really heavy flak. There was a Lancaster above and to the left of us, and suddenly it was just a great big ball of black smoke. Alf, I think instinctively, moved to the right and dived slightly.

It was so close but we heard no noise, and there was no disturbance in the airflow, and yet a Lancaster had disappeared into a cloud of black smoke. It was so close yet we felt no disturbance or noise.

We leveled off and continued to the target where the master bomber had clearly marked the target. We dropped our load and turned and dived away, scurrying home as fast as we could. Fortunately, there were no further incidents, and we landed safely.

On the 6th March we were sent to Rheine Salzbergen, the third op in three consecutive days. However, it was a five and a half hours flight of very calm and uneventful flying, which we all enjoyed.

CHAPTER 9

THE DAMN COOKIE

Two days later on March 7th, our next operation was our second night trip, and fortunately this time it was not raining. When I looked at the map in briefing I saw the ribbon going a long way into the heart of Germany, and at first I thought we were going to Berlin. However when the target was identified it was Dessau, a nine and a half hour trip. We were told that this was to be a very big raid with probably best part of 1,000 bombers in all.

Fortunately, we were the first squadron in the raid, so we had the leading position in a large number of aircraft. With no one in front of you, half of your fear of collision is gone. Our only concern was those alongside of us, and even they were slightly behind. We had been told that previous raids reported heavy flak concentrations around the city and also on both the way in and the way out.

We took off at dusk so were able to formate, we were number two and reserve leader. Our intention was to fly in formation for as long as possible, i.e. as long as we could see each other. Fortunately, it was a clear night and we were able to stay in formation almost all the way to the target. When we got there the master bomber was just starting to mark the target area and we were able to go straight in and drop our bombs.

I was watching them go through my little door and I could see each bomb dropping toward the flares. When the last of them had gone I kept watching the cookie, but it just stayed there!

I called out that we had a 'Hung up cookie.' I closed the bomb bay inspection door and went up to the cockpit and found my toolbox.

'Toolbox' was a fancy name for it! I only had a hammer, a screwdriver, pliers, a roll of insulation tape, and a torch.

We were still at 19,000 feet and I remembered that the cookie clamp, which held the bomb, was in the middle of the bomb bay. Therefore, the access panel to the hand release was in the middle of the rest bay above. Not Heated! In fact, it was at about minus 20 degrees.

I found my silk and woolen gloves, and taking an oxygen extension pipe, went back to the rest bay area. Using my torch, I lifted up the cover panel and taking the screwdriver tried to lever up the release lever. It was firmly stuck. I tried banging it with the hammer and then prying it up again to no avail.

I was finding it extremely cold, but my shivering had to be put up with, and I tried the hammer again.

I suddenly thought, 'There's an axe somewhere!'

I remembered the axe was hanging on the wall a little further down the fuselage. The axe was cast steel and the head had a blade on one side and a spike on the other. I collected it and started hammering the lever with the axe. I tried to lever up the handle with the spike but I could not shift it. All my efforts were in vain.

I paused and looked again at the retaining mechanism. It was held on to the main spar with four bolts. I did not have a spanner, so I attacked them with the axe. I don't know what really happened, but suddenly the bracket splintered and the claw holding the bomb dropped through the bomb doors and the cookie disappeared.

I went back into the cockpit and Alf said, 'Well done' and then with a concerned look said, 'You look like a ghost.' Bob came up from his place and said I looked terrible and I, still shivering, said, 'I'm alright.'

Alf had put the aircraft into a long shallow dive and said we'll get down to a lower altitude and a warmer temperature, and you can have a couple of blankets on the rest bed. I lay on Bob's couch with blankets over me shivering, until Charlie said we were over France. Bob meanwhile was keeping track of the fuel situation. When Alf said we were down to ten thousand feet, Bob took me back to the rest bed and covered me with blankets.

I slept most of the way back, but roused myself when I heard Charlie say to Alf we were getting close to base. I went back out to the cockpit and took up my usual duties for landing. After we landed and got back to dispersal, Bob helped me out and fortunately, we had a crew bus to take us to debriefing.

I have no recollection of what happened next until I woke up in the base hospital. Apparently I collapsed, they had to carry me into the debriefing room. The officer in charge called an ambulance and had me taken to the hospital.

I had two days rest in hospital. It appears I was suffering from exposure, at least that's what they said. I must admit the nurses of Queen Alexandra's Nursing Service spoilt me rotten. When I got back to the billet Bob was the only one there, and said, 'Thanks Ron, we've had a couple of days off thanks to you not being around.'

The next day we did a daylight trip to Datteln, followed by what turned out to be a unique daylight operation for the whole of the war. We went to Bocholt, deep into Germany, with an experimental bomb load. We had the usual 'Cookie' but the rest of the bomb bay was filled with incendiary bombs. It was an uneventful trip there and we were, for a change, late in the formation.

When we arrived the town was just a huge column of smoke extending up to over 10,000 feet and still rising. The master bomber directed us away from the original target and he marked a new target for us to bomb. It was later revealed that the town was virtually wiped out.

For once we had a conscience. Dropping incendiaries in daylight just didn't seem right. It was Charlie, who said to Alf, 'It is somehow different to be one of a large number of aircraft dropping bombs at night when you cannot see the result. But to drop incendiaries in daylight is very different.'

Alf replied that because we dropped bombs at night we were remote from the action, and it was as if we had no responsibility for our actions, we were just one of a large stream of aircraft. In daylight, and particularly to drop incendiaries, was emphasizing what we were doing.

Alf said, 'This is war and the Nazis have no scruples, so why should we.' That ended the discussion.

We said that none of us were superstitious, so when our thirteenth op came around we treated it just like any other. It was a daylight trip and were to fly in HA/M Mike. Strange! M is the thirteenth letter of the alphabet. 218 Squadron were to lead the operation and we were in the front Vic of three, the reserve leader.

We were on our way to Dortmund and we had crossed the French border into Germany when an ME 109 appeared behind and above us.

The Operations Record Book account of the mission to Dessau, March 7/8, 1945. Above the name of F/O R. Cowley is his Australian service number. Take-off was at 17:12 and landing at 02:31, 9 hr 19 min. With permission from The National Archives.

Alf's Logbook page showing his 11th op, the night mission to Dessau, 9 hr 20 min.

Norman and Pete both spotted the fighter and yelled out, but as we were in a big formation there was no room to corkscrew. Norman and Pete were both belting away with their guns and yelling what the fighter was doing.

The fire from all the Lancasters' turrets was quite intense but the fighter seemed to have a charmed life. He made a couple of passes from above us right to left, quickly turned and came in again from the right (my side) from quite high up.

The fighter sped towards us and suddenly there were flashes from the front edges of his wings and a spattering of cannon shells. Holes appeared in our wing tip, moving across the wing toward the engines. Fortunately, they missed the engine and didn't penetrate to the fuel tanks.

We were apparently not seriously damaged as we flew on without any problems. When we approached the target, the flak was intense and we saw two Lancs go down in flames. However, we were O.K. and dropped our bombs. Alf turned sharply, diving away to starboard and left the formation behind. Alf and Charlie had a brief discussion on the route we should take, and Alf said that the North Sea was the nearest way out of Germany so let's try that way.

Charlie gave Alf a course, which would take us to the North Sea and safety, so we kept diving to maintain a good speed and reached the coast fairly quickly. We had encountered no flak en route but at the coast there was a really heavy burst. Charlie said to Alf, 'I told you there would be flak at the coast.' Alf said that we had got through it so it was no problem. We crossed the North Sea without incident and landed at base and found that we were the first back.

For once we did not have to wait for transport back to the debriefing room and were able to take our pick of which table to go to. We described our flight, and as there were no incidents we were out quickly. We headed for the briefing room where we dropped our parachutes and flying clothing and made our way to the mess.

CHAPTER 10

LEAVE

We were stood down for three days and Alf, who had bought an old banger of a car, said he had obtained some petrol from Chiefy, and asked if we would all like to go to Newmarket for the day. Aircraft fuel is 100 octane, whereas car engines use 60, so the ground staff would dilute it, but never let on. No one was supposed to have petrol from the dispersal, but typical of Alf Cowley, he always had a way. Very few people had cars on the station.

We readily agreed, and the following day five of us squeezed into his car and went to the races. I had never been to a racecourse in my life, nor even looked at a racing paper. Fortunately, Bob was very patient and explained it all to me. He saw that I didn't lose too much money on the horses. It was a fantastic day.

The following day I was talking to one of the WAAFs who worked in the mess, an attractive young lady and asked her out. I said we could go into Bury St Edmunds and see a film and have a drink, and she readily agreed. So the next day I had a really pleasant day with her and we agreed to do it again. However, later in the mess I was grabbed by a couple of aircrew types and told I was a nitwit.

'Why?' I asked innocently.

'You took out Chop Lill!'

It seems that every station on Bomber command had a 'Chop Lill,' a girl who was unfortunate enough to lose her boyfriends on raids.

Many flyers were very superstitious, and this sort of situation was always greatly exaggerated. It appeared that the WAAF I took out was called this by a lot of airmen who believed the story that several of the chaps who took her out were killed.

I thought this was outrageous and talked to Alf, who surprised me by saying 'Don't take chances.' I went to see this young lady, but before I could say a word, she told me that she knew what everyone was saying, and that she had applied for a posting away from Chedburgh. In a few days she had gone, but I still felt guilty for a while.

I had a problem living on my money. Before I joined up my mother and I discussed how much I was going to get paid and how much I would need. I was extremely ignorant of this subject, having only lived at home and lived a quiet life. I went dancing once or twice a week with two friends I had met at the Regent ballroom in Grangetown, Cardiff. We used to have a pint in the pub before the dance and would usually try to take a girl home after the dance. I did not smoke in those days, so there was nothing to spend money on except for the odd pint.

When I joined the Air Force, I thought I would not have much to spend money on, particularly in training. On promotion to sergeant I received the princely sum of £3.00 per week, paid fortnightly, with £2 being sent home by the R.A.F. to my mother, ostensibly to be saved in a bank for my return to civvy street. Unfortunately, my mother 'forgot' this arrangement and thought the money was hers to spend.

We had to report to a large hangar where two officers would be sat at a table facing the large area. We would be standing in a large group facing them with a large gap between. One of the officers would call out A's and all the airmen with surnames beginning with A would move forward and queue at the desk. It proceeded through the alphabet and being W, I always had a long wait.

At 218 Squadron Charlie, Pete and Mac were never around in spare periods and as Norman didn't drink, he rarely came to the mess; there was just Bob and me to while away the time together. We only drank beer, and not a lot of that, but it was very much cheaper in the mess than at the local pub. Added to which, the mess was a very comfortable and well-decorated place due to the sponsorship by the Gold Coast.

We rarely went to Stradishall as it was not as good as our mess and it was a bus journey we did not enjoy, particularly in the winter and in the dark.

We were granted six days leave every six weeks whilst on active duty (being available for flying was active duty), and we all left the station. Alf and Mac went into London as Australia House provided accommodation and leave facilities for all Australian personnel. Charlie and Pete spent the time with their wives in Bury St. Edmunds, and Norman and Bob went home which was Lancashire and Yorkshire respectively.

When going on leave, I caught a train from Bury St. Edmunds to St. Pancras, crossed London to Paddington, and caught a train to Cardiff. To travel on leave we were given a railway warrant, which provided a return ticket for the journey home. I spent my leaves alone as Bill Ruddock was now in the army as was Alan, and Stan had joined the Merchant Navy so was away somewhere on a steam ship.

I traveled light as I only took a change of undies, a shirt and socks. At home, the days were boring as I had nothing to do and no one to do it with, but the evenings were great. I have to admit those three stripes and a brevy worked wonders with the girls. Dance partners were many, and taking them home was a natural follow on. It was always a speedy dispatch at the doorstep however, unless I was lucky enough to get a brief kiss.

The days however, were a problem if my father was in, and would always finish up with a row. My mother was a gem and would do anything for me, which annoyed my father. It always ended with me walking out and going for a long walk.

Weekends were not bad as I could go and watch Cardiff play rugby, just across the road. By this time my parents were living in Penarth Road, the main road from Cardiff to Penarth, and only around the corner from where I was born in Taff Embankment. I have to admit that I was usually glad to go back to the Squadron.

There was an American aerodrome on the other side of Bury St. Edmunds, about the same distance away as we were. One evening in a pub in Bury, Bob and I ran into a few American aircrew. We had a rousing evening with them and they were so generous we had a job to buy a round. We knew that they only did daylight operations, but stayed off the subject in order not to offend them.

About two weeks later, some American officer aircrew visited us at Chedburgh. We entertained them in the mess and had a great evening. Officers and other ranks all 'mucked in' and the result was an invitation for us to visit them at their 'drome.' Unfortunately for us, we were flying on the night the visit was fixed for, and so we never made it.

Later, the Americans contacted us and asked us to arrange a party for the local children. They said that they would supply all the food and drink. They also provided the entertainment; several of them dressed up and the children had a ball. They brought chocolates and sweets for the children, the like of which most of them had never seen, especially with the rationing we were experiencing.

Relations were with the Americans were great from then on, and there were no problems between us in Bury St. Edmunds.

CHAPTER 11

OUR LAST FEW MISSIONS

Our next operation on March 19th was scheduled as a daylight trip to Gelsenkirchen, yet again, and when we ventured out into the dawn light for breakfast, it was throwing it down. We dived back for capes (only officers had mackintoshes!) and ran to the mess.

Things went smoothly until we got to the briefing room where we learnt that due to the terrible weather, the op was postponed. We were to remain available, as the operation would be rescheduled as soon as the weather allowed. So we all trooped back to the mess and hung around waiting.

Eventually we were told that we were going and it would be a night trip. We went to briefing at 6:00 p.m. but there were delays and finally we started taxiing 'P Popsy' down the peri track at about 8:00 p.m. in torrential rain, which made visibility very difficult. Bob had to go down into the nose to guide us along. I was watching the temperature gauges and the port outer was getting hot. I pointed it out to Alf, and he said to give it a few more minutes.

Five minutes later the port outer was very hot and I told Alf we should report it straight away. He contacted the tower and they said we were to hang on. Within a few minutes we were told to shut the engines down and vacate the aircraft. We were ordered to run to the other side of the airfield where we were to board the reserve

Lancaster, which was being started up by the ground crew, and told to get airborne as soon as possible.

Tractors appeared from nowhere and 'P Popsy' was dragged unceremoniously off the peri track, allowing the other Lancs to proceed. It was still pouring with rain and we had to run straight across the soggy grass airfield in flying kit and Mae Wests, carrying all our gear in the pitch dark. By the time we got to 'O Oboe' we were soaked, muddy and out of breath, but there was no time for moaning. The ground crew was there urging us, 'Get your fingers out and get going!'

As all the other aircraft had departed, we went the shortest route, the wrong way around the peri track. We were much nearer the runway in that direction and there was now no one left but us. We got into the air as quickly as we could.

We soon settled down and everyone was moaning about being soaking wet and uncomfortable. Alf suddenly said, 'Quiet all of you, the trip has to be done and so make the best of it.' We went after all the others to Gelsenkirchen, yet again.

As we were late, we were joining the later aircraft of the stream and since it was dark, our only way to see the others was to look for their exhaust gases, which were very red. However there were fairings over the manifolds to hide them from the fighters so it was very difficult.

Alf decided that we would go along the track as detailed, but at a slightly lower level and hope that the background of the flames at the target would expose the others so we could climb up to their level. If we had proceeded on below them, we would have been in the path of their bombs when they were dropped.

Things went along normally until we approached the German border where the weather cleared. Charlie told me to 'Start windowing' and I duly collected the bundles of Aluminium and started to push them out.

The Germans had radar and it located aircraft and notified the anti-aircraft artillery batteries where we were and at what height. To upset the radar reception we (that is, the British 'boffins') invented a device that upset the radar images. It consisted of thin Aluminium foil strips about 10 inches long by one and a half inches wide, approximately twenty to a bundle. They were packed into parcels and stored at the rear of the bomb aimer's compartment.

It was the flight engineers job to collect them and put them out a bundle at a time counting seconds between, in accordance with the instructions received from the wireless operator. Where he got the instructions from I do not know, but someone somewhere had the information to pass to all the aircraft flying in that area.

Looking back I could see a sea of aluminum pieces reflecting what little light there was as the adjacent aircraft dropped their bundles too. I realised that although we had been delayed in our take-off, we were probably catching up with the main stream of what we learned the next day, was a force of 1,000 bombers all targeting Gelsenkirchen. This explained the volume of 'window' being pushed out. 'Window' was supposed to provide a screen to protect us from the German radar.

Some protection!

We were caught in a searchlight beam and it was brighter than daylight. It is a frightening experience to be in the cockpit of an aircraft, illuminated beyond daylight level with shells bursting all around you.

Suddenly flak started bursting around us, and we were showered with shrapnel. Alf took evasive action and we broke free with no one hurt, fortunately. We resumed our original course and climbed back up to 20,000 feet. We saw one or two planes' exhausts and felt better for the company.

We approached the target and I got down into the nose compartment with Bob, opened the flap and watched the cookie and incendiaries drop. Seeing them all go was a relief, as incendiaries were notorious for hanging up. I went back to my post and shut the bomb doors and we turned for home. An uneventful trip home was greatly appreciated for it was a nine-hour flight in the dark, which made it seem even longer.

Operation 15 was a day trip to Bocholt, which was only a four and three quarter hour trip. It can best be described as a dawdle.

A short while ago I was talking to Alf Cowley on the telephone and told him that I was writing a book of my wartime experiences. He was very interested and we had a long chat. Sometime later I received in the mail a letter from Alf enclosing an account of the raid we did on the night of 9/10th April 1945 to Kiel. I think his version should take priority so here is Alf's account.

> We flew 'HA/X' (the designation of the aircraft) on this raid. The briefed target was the submarine pens and the inner harbour area of Kiel. PFF (Path Finder Force) marked the area to be bombed. No specific mention of the 'Scheer' was made in the pre-flight briefing.
>
> It was a clear night. The searchlights and flak were very active as were the fighters. We had a good run to the aiming point and the

'cookie' was the last bomb to be released. The camera mounted in the underside of the nose was timed, in theory, to expose when the cookie hit the target. For many reasons this did not happen. It was necessary to keep the aircraft on a straight and level path to ensure the camera photographed the actual explosion of our cookie, when it exploded. Bob set the altitude and airspeed so that the photograph occurred when the explosion took place. The flash of the camera was clearly seen in the nose being reflected in the glass of the nose dome.

It was chaotic in the target area with a lot of aircraft trying to get in line with a small target, at least it was small to us but when we saw the Admiral Scheer it was obviously a large ship.

By a freakish chain of events the battleship exploded right when our cookie hit the target. Even from 20,000 feet, it was a sight, an almost blinding flash and the ship turned right over exposing her keel.

A number of cookies and incendiaries had hit her in a very short time, which blew the side out of her. Our camera recorded the actual exposure and was sent to Bomber Command for analysis of evidence of the success of the raid.

As we proceeded toward home the crew was jubilant until I told them that celebration could wait until we got home.

When we went into the briefing room after an uneventful trip home, the Security guys said, 'You look happy.' We all smiled and said, 'We just sank the Admiral Scheer!'

There was a cheer and we were congratulated, but I told them that there were one or two others there as well. We all laughed and sat down and went through the full debriefing. Groupy was there and said, 'There'll be one hell of a party tomorrow night.' And so there was.

The next morning the national dailies of both the U.K. and Australia were full of praise for the R.A.F., who had sunk the Admiral Scheer in Kiel Harbour. The B.B.C. and the English press also sang our praises and for once we were in the limelight.

The Daily Sketch

THURSDAY, APRIL 12, 1945

The Kill: Picture From The Air

The German pocket battleship Admiral Scheer lying upside down in the inner dockyard basin at Kiel after the R.A.F. Bomber Command attack.

German Pocket Battleship Scheer Sunk By R.A.F. Bomb

THE pocket-battleship Admiral Scheer has been sunk by R.A.F. Lancasters at Kiel, her home base, the Air Ministry announced last night.

Air photographs show the Scheer lying in the inner dock in the dockyard basin almost completely upside down. Two days before the Lancasters' attack on Monday night reconnaissance had shown her moored in the basin.

She had been driven to Kiel when Gdynia was first threatened by the Russians and had previously played an important part in the defence and evacuation of German pockets of resistance on the Baltic coast.

Many of the air crews reported a violent explosion which they thought at the time was caused by a hit on either a ship or an ammunition dump.

Said Flt.-Lieut. Albert N. Marshall, a pilot from Runcorn, Cheshire:

"A sheet of flame rose high in see the docks and the port very clearly. The whole target area seemed to be a mass of flames, with the fires starting from two aiming points and merging into one."

Sergt. F. Jenkins, of Brisbane, Australia, said: "I saw an explosion fling debris many hundreds of feet into the air and, in the glow of the fires, I saw six ships. Dense clouds of smoke were coming up."

The Germans described the Scheer as a vessel of 10,000 tons, but this figure was probably given to disarm suspicion. It is certain that her displacement was more than 12,000 tons, says the Air Ministry.

She was one of Germany's two remaining pocket-battleships, the other being the Lutzow.

The third was the inglorious Graf Spee, which was scuttled to avoid battle in the River Plate in December, 1939.

Scheer survived an attack in April, 1940, when she was torpedoed by the submarine Spearfish.

She was 600ft. long and carried six 11in. and eight 5.9in. guns among other weapons, as well as two planes.

Early in the war the Scheer sank a number of British ships, including the 10,000-ton Doric Star in the South Atlantic.

Early in 1941 she broke out into the Atlantic and raided shipping. She was operating with a vessel disguised as the American s.s. Dixie, which was used for supply purposes and also as a prison ship.

She was the ship which during the Spanish War, shelled Almeria on May 29, 1937, as a reprisal for the bombing of the Deutschland. Then 3,000 people were rendered homeless and the damage was placed at £200,000.

We sank the Admiral Scheer!

Alf kept this copy of the *Daily Mail* for 60 years. Alf's handwriting at the top reads 'We were on the last raid on Berlin by Lancasters on the night of 14 April 1945 -- 9-10 hours. The night before we went to Kiel 5-6 hours. Came home on 3 motors.

Our 18th operation was a prestigious one for us, as it was the night we went to Berlin, which took nine and a half hours there and back. We were told at briefing that this was a maximum effort and every squadron had been briefed to get every possible aircraft in the air.

The Operations Record Book account of the mission to Berlin on the night of 14/15th April, 1945. After the description of the raid, it reads "Cookie had to be manually released on built up area to West of Potsdam owing to build up. My Navigator was ill all the way out but stuck to his post and made a good job of it." (With permission, The National Archives.)

Again we were fortunate in leading the operation, so had no problems with numbers of aircraft in our vicinity. It was a quiet flight out until we crossed the French/German border. Word had got out and the flak was very heavy and soon we had night fighters attacking the stream. We were very fortunate, as we were not troubled by fighters, only flak and searchlights. As we approached Berlin, the ground was illuminated by flames and flares.

We heard the master bomber say 'Bomb on Green.' A mass of green flares exploded under us and we did as we were instructed and according to Bob, dropped our bombs right in the middle. The flak was the heaviest we had ever encountered. As soon as we thought we were out of the flak, there were night fighters all over the place. We lost a lot of planes that night, but we were lucky and came home with a damaged aircraft, but not seriously, and fortunately for us, not a damaged crew.

It was morning when we landed and we were waiting around for the crew bus when a Lanc came in to land, overshot and went round again. When it came in the second time it seemed to go down the whole length of the runway at a height of about four feet and as it went over the fence at the end of the runway, it nose dived into the ground. The aircraft exploded. The rear turret broke away from the fuselage on impact and the rear gunner walked away unhurt.

Although the emergency crews worked hard they could not get anyone else out. The pilot was Flight Lieutenant (Tubby) Spiers. He and his crew were on the last trip of their second tour, their 50th operation. It was later established that they had a 250lb bomb hung up and it exploded in the crash.

The Squadron was very demoralized for a while and Tubby was sorely missed, as he was much liked. He had survived so many operations that he was a mascot.

The mess was very depressed for days, as most of us had never seen an actual crash and this one was one of our aircraft. Three of the crew were Warrant Officers and were well-known in our mess.

We had a rest for five days and then it was Operation 19 to Munich. It was a six and three quarter hour trip in daylight and I am pleased to relate that it was uneventful.

That raid was the thirtieth for Warrant Officer Jameson and his crew and they were the first crew to complete a tour of 30 operations for two months. The Station Commander announced that to celebrate this we were to stand down for 48 hours, and there was to be a party in the sergeants' mess for all aircrew. The Ground staff were also to have a party in the airman's mess. There was still 'class' in the R.A.F.

We were not into the wine, so the beer flowed freely that evening and after dinner was a 'Reliego' knock out competition with each crew taking part. We had played this once before so we knew what to expect. We performed a lot better but were a long way from winning. It was a hell of a party and ended with the usual sing-song with the traditional Air Force versions dominating. Wisely we were off the next day!

Operation 20 was my second where I joined another crew. I only found out later that the engineer of this crew was on his second tour and suddenly could not face it any more. This happened from time to time, and as far as we aircrew were concerned, it was perfectly reasonable and quite understandable.

However, the R.A.F. had a very different view and anyone refusing to fly was immediately removed from the Squadron, their brevies or wings, were removed, and they were demoted back to the rank of AC2, Airman 2nd class, the lowest of the low. They were branded as LMF, 'Lacking Moral Fiber,' which was another way of saying they were cowards.

They were posted to other stations and given 'other duties' to perform. I thought then, and still think now, that it was a disgusting way to treat men. Many of them, such as the flight engineer I replaced, had served bravely for a long time. I bet the people who thought up this treatment had not flown on an operation.

The pilot was a warrant officer and was a superb pilot but he and his crew had only done three trips together as his aircraft had been badly shot up on a previous trip. They had lost both gunners and the wireless op.

No wonder the engineer went LMF!

I was probably their good luck charm because we had a very easy daylight trip of 6 hours, which I particularly enjoyed. The visibility was brilliant and there were hardly any clouds. The W/O pilot even let me have quite a long spell at the controls. Gerry must have had a day off because we saw no fighters and very little flak.

Operation 21 was a daylight raid to Regensburg on the 20th April, a very long trip since it was a town at the southern border of Germany, almost on the French border. We were reserve leader so we were No. 2 in the formation, immediately on the right shoulder of the leader.

We were routed deeply into France to escape the worst of the flak sites. For the first part it was almost

10/10th cloud and we traveled undisturbed. The 'Met' men referred to cloud thickness by tenths. That is, no cloud is 0/10th and total cloud is 10/10ths.

As we went further south, it was as if the war was actually over. The clouds disappeared, and the sun was shining. The scenery was green and beautiful, and one could imagine that we were on a pleasure trip. Deep into France the snow-capped Alps appeared on the horizon.

Pete suddenly came on the intercom and said, 'I can clearly see right back as far as the horizon and it is full of aircraft. The weather has never been quite this perfect before, and so to see the extent of the formation so clearly is unbelievable. The Germans must be terrified', he said. Alf interrupted him and said 'Cut it out, we are here to do a job, let's get on with it.'

As we continued south, it just became more beautiful as the Alps grew in size and the scenery became clearer. The tops of the mountains were clad in pure white snow and below it were several shades of green with the trees beginning to show more clearly. Alf sensed my fascination and said, 'I said it once, this is not a pleasure outing, we've come to do a job. Let's get on with it.' Suitably chastised, I got on with my job.

Soon the town of Regensburg appeared and the master bomber came on directing us toward the target, which was clearly visible on the right of the town. It was a large industrial area, which eased my conscience, which was troubling me that day. However we did drop the bombs, and could see the effects. It was war after all. They started it and we were finishing it.

It was a long trip home and we used our height to maximum effect to save fuel. When we saw the English coast, we were very relieved. For the first time in a while we did not see an aircraft go down. However, I must say that being in the front and looking forward most of the time, we were not likely to.

When we landed and got to our dispersal, Chiefy was waiting for me. When I finished my 'end of trip tasks' I climbed out, and he was at the steps. He asked me how it had gone, and I told him that everything was great. He said, 'How about the starboard outer?' I said that it was fine, no trouble at all. Chiefy said that he was concerned because it had been troublesome on its last flight. This was typical of their concern for us.

CHAPTER 12

RELIEF OF THE DUTCH
"The Manna Drops"

For a short while all activity stopped and then suddenly we were called for a special briefing. The Dutch were absolutely starving and the Germans had agreed that we could do an airlift operation to Rotterdam. No action would be taken against us as long as we stuck rigidly to the agreed route and height, and made only one pass of the dropping zone. Officially, the war was still on but there was little action taking place.

We were given very strict instructions to fly on the 29th April, 1945 and were to drop food panniers at Rotterdam in a marked field. Our crew were to be the leaders of our squadron, and our squadron would lead all the other aircraft. Charlie had a special briefing on the exact location of the field and time of commencement.

Every available aircraft was to take part, in as many squadrons as possible. It was a great honour to be the leaders of such an operation. A further honour was that we were to fly in HA/U Uncle, a Lancaster that had completed 100 operations for 218 Squadron.

The food, all in tins or secure parcels, was packed into large panniers, which were loaded into the bomb bay. The ground crew put as much in each pannier as they could and shut the bomb bay doors quickly so as not to lose one little bit.

We took off late morning and flew at 500 feet all the way, which we enjoyed because we all loved low-level stuff. We crossed the coast and the German guns were all pointed at us and followed us in our flight. They didn't open fire but it was very threatening, particularly since at such a low level they were clearly visible.

We turned toward Rotterdam and Charlie joined Bob in the nose with his map. He had been given a very large-scale map of the town, with the School and its playing field clearly marked. He guided us right over the town and the school and I think every member of the population was out to greet us and in their own way, say thank you.

Prior to going, we as a crew, had collected sweets, chocolates and cigarettes, and made a parcel with a homemade parachute. As we flew over the field and dropped the panniers, I threw our parcel out of my window.

When I checked the bomb bay I found that two panniers had not dropped. As we turned back north, we all agreed that we didn't want to take food home, so we turned and joined in the stream and tried again to drop the panniers. As we turned to try and go around again the Germans spotted that we had been before and opened fire on us.

The last panniers had still not dropped but we shut up shop and turned for home. Suddenly there was another burst of rifle fire and the aircraft shuddered and the nose climbed. It took both Alf and me and all our strength to get the control column forward and level the aircraft. We managed to push it forward so that the aircraft was level again. Alf called Bob to relieve me, so that I could go and investigate.

When I got to the rear, the fuselage was a mess as the trimming tab control wires were all over the place. The shells had completely severed the wires, so the control surfaces were unmanageable. My training at St. Athan came to the fore and I was able to identify the elevator wires and by winding out the excess, I was able to join them up with insulation tape.

I then repeated the procedure for the rudder cables but there was no excess cable to join them up. So I called Norman down from his turret and identified each cable. I connected up his intercom with an extension so that he could talk to the cockpit. My idea was for Alf to call down instructions from the cockpit, 'Pull Left' or 'Pull Right' as required, and Norm was to pull the appropriate wire.

This was difficult flying for Alf as he moved instinctively and stopping to tell someone else to do something upset his timing. We conveyed our difficulty to Control at base, and we were diverted to Woodbridge to ease the landing problem.

Woodbridge was an emergency base in Kent, close to the coast and provided an early haven for aircraft in trouble, which we clearly were. However, with the great extra length of that runway, and Pete and Norman pulling the wires carefully, we put old 'Uncle' down.

When we shut everything down, our last action was to open the bomb bay doors to vent the hydraulic system. This I did, to a chorus of yells—the remaining food panniers had dropped onto the tarmac. The food had spilled out and the ground crew was 'delighted' at the mess they had to clear up.

Date	Aircraft Type & Number	Crew	Duty	Time Up	Time Down	Details of Sortie or Flight
1945 29th April	LANCASTER I & III. AIR. 434185. U. M. 223 ROTTERDAM FOOD DROP	P/O E.R. Cawley. Sgt. Lane, G. AUS. 437350. W/S. McNair, R. Sgt. Davies, R. Sgt. Green, E. P/S Belt, M. Sgt. Washurton, R.	Capta in. Navigator. Wop/Air. Air Bomber. M.U. Gunner. R. Gunner. Flt. Engr.	13.06.	15.46	Dropped two packs on 1st run and one on the second. Two packs were brought back due to hang up. Aircraft was fired on by rifle 2000 yards south of the dropping area. Damage to elevator tabs, rudder, hydraulic pipe to mid under turret and main former. Aircraft diverted to Woodridge. Good concentration of packages in area.

The official Operations Record Book entry for the first of the 'Manna Drops.' to Rotterdam on April 29th, 1945. The record reads "Dropped two packs on 1st run and one on the second. Two packs were brought back due to hang up. Aircraft was fired on by rifle 2000 yards south of the dropping area. Damage to elevator tabs, rudder, hydraulic pipe to mid under turret and main former. Aircraft diverted to Woodbridge. Good concentration of packages in area." (With permission, The National Archives.)

We had to hang around for some hours until a truck arrived from Chedburgh to take us back. Supposedly, there was to be no stopping at pubs as we had to get back before dark. However, we were so uncomfortable in the back of the truck that we hammered on the cab until they stopped at a pub where refreshments were obtained.

Alf's Log Page for the 'Manna Drops' to The Hague, May 1945.

On arrival at Chedburgh our merry state was not noticed as it was late, and everyone was relieved to know we were O.K. and so had gone to bed.

* * *

That was the first of our four 'Manna' drops, one to Rotterdam and three to The Hague. In total 6,500 tons of food were dropped and saved many lives. To this day the Dutch remember these drops and still hold a ceremony each year to express their gratitude.

Many years later at a special commemoration, the Dutch authorities traced Alf to his home in Australia and invited him to come to their ceremony. He was asked to invite the rest of his crew but unfortunately we had all lost touch and so he went alone.

There was a huge crowd in the centre of Rotterdam and during the mayor's speech there was a commotion caused by a gentleman forcing his way through to Alf. When he finally made it he asked, 'Are you Alf Cowley?' Alf said 'yes' and the gentleman said, 'I was the little boy who picked up your parcel!'

Then he produced the note we had written and included with the sweets and cigarettes that we had parachuted down to them!

There were many speeches but finally Alf and the Mayor led the V.I.P.'s to a hotel where they had lunch. After a splendid meal there were more speeches and then Alf and the Mayor were taken to the airport. There Alf was invited to take the Mayor and some of his officials for a flight around Rotterdam. Apparently they enjoyed it so much they wouldn't let him land until they were nearly out of petrol.

In 2005 I heard of an event called the 'Cheese Run,' which was held in the R.A.F. Home in Storrington, a village about tem miles North of where we live. It was a celebration to mark the dropping of food to the Dutch in 1945. Margaret and I turned up and found that it was being organized by the R.A.F. with invited guests, some of whom were quite senior R.A.F. officers.

However, the organizing committee, that is the officers, were in a private room. Outside on the terrace were a lot of Dutch people who had come over for the event. There were also a few spectators, locals who had learned of the event. There was one other gentleman, who I singled out, and he turned out to be the only other person there who had actually flown on the 'Manna Drops.'

We were ignored by the committee and excluded from the room where the main luncheon was. However, I had with me some photographs of 'HA/U Uncle,' the Lancaster that led the operation, with our crew on board. There was a guy there from the B.B.C. together with a reporter who was also out with us. They showed great interest in us veterans and in the photographs, and the latter were shown on TV that night.

There was also a display by two helicopters that flew low over the grounds and then landed, and the pilots joined us. One of them asked me if I had been to the 'R.A.F. Battle of Britain Memorial Flight' H.Q. at Conningsby in Lincolnshire. I said that I had not, and they said that I should telephone Squadron Leader Pinner, who would be delighted to show me around.

The following June Margaret and I attended the 218 Squadron reunion in Bury St. Edmunds and immediately after, we went up to Conningsby. The Memorial Flight had a large hangar with several Spitfires at one end and at the other end was the Lancaster. We were met by Squadron Leader Pinner, who greeted us warmly, and showed us all around.

Margaret stood under the Lancaster and her face was a picture. She found the aircraft extremely menacing, nothing like the 6" photograph with the smiling, friendly crew stood under 'HA/U Uncle' in our hall.

The last remaining Lancaster that is still flying at the 'Battle of Britain Memorial Flight' housed at RAF Conningsby, Lincolnshire. (Photograph, Margaret Warburton.)

We walked around and were invited to climb into the Lancaster. I went in and made my way up to my old position in the front of the cockpit area. I opened what used to be my window and peered out. I turned to Margaret and said, 'This is where I used to stand for 6–8 hours.' She said, 'Isn't is dark?'

Squadron Leader Pinner was smiling and said, 'Obviously brings back a lot of memories.' I was almost overcome as the memories flooded back.

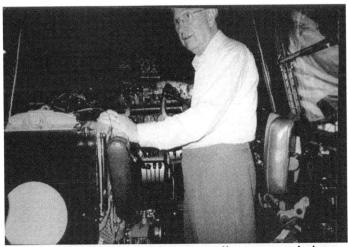

Reliving memories 50 years later—standing once again in my working position, where I stood for so many hours.

*   *   *

The last Manna Drop was to The Hague on May 7th, 1945. Then it was announced that the Germans had surrendered and that an armistice had been signed at Luneburg Heath, Potsdam, near Berlin. I was so glad that we had not flattened that area when we bombed it.

The next day, May 8th, 1945 was declared a National Holiday, called V.E. Day, or Victory in Europe Day. We had a party in the Mess, with each mess having its own 'do,' and everyone enjoyed a great celebration. A memorable day was had by all.

There was a definite lull in activities, and so we were all stood down and given seven days leave. The atmosphere was like a holiday, with everyone so glad that the war was over.

I went home to Cardiff, and for a while was in a happy mood, but after a few days things died down and I had nothing to do and was bored.

Out walking one day, I found myself near the Cardiff City Hall and stood a little bemused as to how I had ended up there. Suddenly, I was approached by a very attractive young lady who said, 'You look worn out, come home with me and have a cup of tea.'

I recognized her as a regular at the Saturday dances so we walked up Whitchurch Road to her home where I had a royal welcome from her mum and dad. I was fed and watered until I was fit to burst. Any hopes I had for the evening were quickly dispelled, however, when she told me she had a date. Still, I had a great evening at the dance.

I was glad to return to Chedburgh and join the crew again. On the 19th May, we went to Woodbridge to pick up 'Uncle.' We went by truck, with Alf comfortable in the front and the rest of us standing up and hanging on in the back. We found 'Uncle' in dispersal and Alf told me to check it out.

I found the local Chiefy and tactfully asked if I might look it over. He grinned.

'That's your job, Son!'

I went round and then checked inside. It was very clean and tidy. We all climbed aboard and flew old 'Uncle' back to Chedburgh, where the ground crew greeted us with cheers.

The next day, we were told that the Squadron was to do some sight-seeing trips. The Big Wigs wanted to see the effect of the bombing and so we did daylight trips taking high-ranking officers on tours of Germany. The first time we approached Cologne they were all speechless, the cathedral stood out on a flat plane of ruins for miles around. The devastation was unbelievable, and so it was as we went around various cities.

We were truly shocked and very guilty at the vast desolation of residential areas in a very large number of cities. I had not seen the after-effects of our bombing before, and it was a shock to me. It made me realize exactly what we had done. However, Norman put it into perspective by saying, 'Well they started it and we finished it.'

As we completed the tour of all the cities that had been targets, we were forced to think about the thousands of homeless Germans who, after all, were as innocent as our population. Of course, it is easy to be wise after the event, but at the time I was too busy worrying about the flak and fighters.

The next priority was the return of the prisoners of war and there was insufficient transport to bring them back, so Bomber Command was asked to do the job. Off we went to Germany to pick them up and bring them home. As the gunners had no duties on these flights, they were put in charge of shepherding the prisoners aboard and seating them on the benches we had put in.

On one trip, we got out in Germany to be greeted by an Army Colonel, who immediately asked who was in charge. Norman moved forward and the Colonel introduced himself and said he was to fly up front with the pilot.

Norman said, 'Yes sir, stand over there and we'll sort it out in a moment.' He then loaded all the squaddies and turned to the Colonel and said 'Right you are Sir, up you get.'

The only place left for him to sit was on the Elsan (the chemical toilet!) in the back of the aircraft. He behaved badly all the way home and swore he would have his revenge on Norman by reporting him immediately when he got back. However we heard no more of this, so the authorities must have decided to take no action.

On May 22nd, we did some practice bombing runs. Why? Neither I nor the others had any idea why, but it was great to fly around and we extended the trip for fun.

On 23rd May, we flew to Dunsford to take a senior officer for a visit to Joivin Court. We left him there and went back later in the day to collect him. We never found out what he did there.

Soon afterwards, the Australians and Canadians were repatriated. When Alf and Mac left, that left the rest of us as an incomplete crew. Since we were to be posted and the squadron disbanded, we naturally had to have a party. Needless to say it was a party to end all parties, and there were some very sore heads the next day.

* * *

218 (Gold Coast) Squadron was disbanded in July 1945 to become a part of history, and the part played by all the British, Canadian and Australian airmen is well recorded, not only in some very good books by journalists, but also in the official Operations Record Books at The National Archives in Kew, London.

Alf's Log Book showing the completion of his "First Tour": 21 sorties, 3 manna drops and 1 exodus. The page was signed by Wing Commander Smith.

HA/U Uncle, our favorite aircraft was one of less than 50 aircraft out of the many thousands of Lancasters of Bomber Command to complete over 100 operations, and was seriously damaged only four times.

Between June 1944 and April 1945, 218 Squadron dropped 8,268 tons of bombs on Germany. Other Squadrons did their share but the cost was enormous. 55,573 airmen of Bomber Command lost their lives.

I enjoyed my flying career very much especially the exciting times, but reflection leaves a guilty conscience for all the damage caused and people killed. I know it was war and that someone had to stand up and fight, but what a terribly pointless waste of human life.

I think of the thousands of aircrew who lost their lives whilst I was at 218. Bomber Command comprised only 7% of the British Armed Forces, yet accounted for 25% of the total casualties of the war.

I consider myself to be one very lucky airman.

* * *

After a 14-day leave spent at home, I returned to find I was posted to Selby in Yorkshire. Chedburgh was relatively deserted, with only a few planes, not many people, and no flying going on. All the personnel from abroad had already left, so I never had a chance to say good bye to Alf and Mac. In fact, the only member of the crew I found was Bob, and I only saw him briefly when he was on his way out with his kit, to go to the station.

There were quite a few ex-aircrew and we were marshaled outside the admin office. There we were given individual postings. I and a few others were posted to Selby in Yorkshire. Much to my surprise, when I got there it was not an aerodrome but a ground staff training camp. We were told that our flying days were over and that we were to help the nation by working on farms until further notice. We would be paid by the farmers on a piece-work basis.

The next morning we were driven by lorry to a farm and I found I was to pick potatoes. I was down on hands and knees, crawling along the furrows, digging my hands into the mucky ground to find the potatoes and put them in bags. We had a brief stop for lunch and carried on until about three o'clock when the lorry returned to take us back to camp.

We were paid by the pound, but it hardly amounted to enough for the night's beer! We were absolutely filthy and could not wait to get in the shower. Great treatment of heroes!

This went on for two weeks, going to a different farm every few days. By this time I had had enough of farming and on the next Monday morning I refused to get on the truck and went to the orderly room to see the station admin officer. I asked what my alternatives were, and he said I could re-muster to a ground trade if I wanted to, or stick to the farming. He was actually very sympathetic, and after a while he suggested that with my history, I should go for a Fitter 2E's course, which would stand me in good stead in 'civvy street.'

This was a course of instruction on aero engines and looked very detailed and interesting. I filled out the necessary form and he said I could hang around until the posting came through. A week later I was sent on leave for seven days and told to report back to Locking Air Force station near Weston Super Mare in Somerset, for my course, which had been approved. I was extremely fortunate as the courses lasted six months and

I had applied just as one was about to start. He also said that my Flight Sergeant's promotion had arrived and gave me two crowns to wear on my sleeves above the stripes.

After a week of dancing and some drinking with much chasing of the ladies, I reported to Locking and was allocated a billet in a Nissen hut, but I had the N.C.O's room at the end, whilst the main hut area was filled with 'A.C. Plonks' as they were called, the lowest rank of the Air Force.

The next morning I had to report to the Chief Training Officer who was an elderly engineering officer of Flight Lieutenant rank. He said that I was going to be in a difficult position as during the day I had to cover up my Flight Sergeant's stripes with an armband, and be a Leading Aircraftman's rank.

When the days training was over I could remove the armband and revert to my proper rank and use the sergeants' mess. This was because the course was intended for low ranking personnel and all the instructors were corporals. 'We can't have you lording it over them now, can we?' he said.

So for six months I endured a repeat of almost all of my Flight Engineer's course on engines, with more emphasis on maintenance, but in very similar surroundings. In the evening I became the Flight Sergeant in charge of the hut, allocating duties and supervising the non-course activities.

Actually, the hut guys were no problem at all, and we got on very well, but the corporal instructors were a shower, and really tried to take it out of me. If there was a dirty job during the day, I got it, and so on right through the course. I did however heed the advice of my superior and did not take revenge in the evening when I out-ranked them.

However, I had the last laugh as I was examined by the chief training officer and not by a corporal, and came out top of the course. It was not very satisfying as I had done 90% of it before, and spent many months flying.

During the course I went home to Cardiff most weekends. One of the Ground Crew Sergeants came from Cardiff and had a car, an old Opel, in which he drove home most weekends. When he found I was from his town, he offered me a lift any time he was going. Saturdays at home became a ritual, with a rugby match in the afternoon and dancing in the evening.

The City Hall in the centre of the city was the best dancehall both for dancing and picking up girls. There was a strict code of no alcohol, and if your breath smelled of drink you were refused admission. So the Celtic ballroom at the bottom of City road became my first choice.

One Saturday night when I had had very little to drink, I was sat in the Celtic ballroom watching the dancers when I saw an attractive girl dancing with a chap who obviously had a false leg. They were doing a rumba and in my conceit, I thought, I can do better than a guy with one leg. So when the next dance started I asked her to dance.

She really did dance well, and was easy to talk to, so I hung on to her for the rest of the evening. When the dance ended we exchanged names, hers was Margaret, and I asked if I could see her home. She said yes! So we strolled arm in arm up City Road to Treharris Street, where she lived. It is a very long street of terraced houses with no front gardens. So she sat on the windowsill of the front room, and I stood on the pavement and we chatted awhile.

I asked if she would like to go to the concert the following evening and she said 'yes.' This was Wales in the late 40's, so there were no dances or even pubs open on Sundays, but there were 'big band' concerts in the Capitol cinema. The next evening quite early, I stood outside the theatre and a tram drew up. A smashing pair of legs appeared under the body of the tram and walked around to my side. Lo and behold, it was Margaret!

We went in to the hall and thoroughly enjoyed the concert, holding hands. Remember, I said this was the 40's and things happened slowly back then. At the end of the concert I walked her home and again we chatted in the street until suddenly the upstairs window opened and a voice said, 'Peggy, is that you?' She said 'Yes, I'll be in now.'

'I thought your name was Margaret,' I said. Her parents and family all called her Peggy, but her name was Margaret. 'That's what I shall call you', I said.

We agreed to meet the next weekend but I was not risking losing her to the one-legged guy, so I suggested the cinema. I am pleased to say the relationship blossomed and I saw her most weekends.

One week my friend's car was in for repair, and I said that I would not be coming over. At the last minute, however, he collected the car and we went to Cardiff. I called at Margaret's house only to find she had gone to the Gaiety cinema, not far away. So I went there and saw an usherette who knew her, as did everyone!

The usherette went up to the balcony, shining her torch around in the middle of the film, much to everyone's annoyance, asking for Margaret Bargery. The usherette finally found her and said 'Ron's downstairs.'

Margaret beat a hasty retreat, accompanied by rude remarks and came down to me, but as she was very embarrassed she was not exactly polite in her greeting. However the evening passed very pleasantly afterwards.

Another Saturday we went to the Gaiety Cinema and went upstairs, always the best seats for Ron, and as we sat down Margaret took off her hat. She was very smart in her dress, and had good taste. Margaret was one of those rare ladies who frequently wore a hat, usually held in place by a large hat-pin. When the hat was removed she usually stuck the pin in the hat until she put it on again. She pushed the pin into the hat, but it would not go through.

After several attempts the hat was placed on my knee and raising the pin aloft, she pushed the pin down hard on the hat. The pin went straight through the hat and into my leg!

With a loud 'OW!' I jumped up, only to be told by the people behind to sit down. Turning around to face them, made the hat turn, and I said 'Can't you see I've got a bloody propeller on my leg?' Fortunately, they thought it funny, and I was in a flyer's uniform, but I wasn't greatly pleased.

I was then sent to Henlow, a large aerodrome, which had been a centre of aviation in peacetime. However there was nothing for us to do except wander around the town and avoid guard duties on the main gate. We were bored to tears but there was nothing we or anyone else could do. Finally someone at the top decided to send all these idle aircrew out to Burma. I still wonder why.

CHAPTER 13

BURMA

I was sent on embarkation leave as I had been posted to Mingaladon in Burma. This was a great surprise because the war in the Far East was over and I could see no point in going out there. However there was no arguing with the R.A.F. I had to go.

Margaret and I had seven days together and things got quite serious. One day we were in Penarth Road, my home and after a good 'snog' we were talking, and suddenly I asked her to marry me. I received a good hug and the answer was yes.

I then confessed that I had some money put away to buy a set of drawing instruments so that I could get a job as a draughtsman when I came home. I guess a ring had greater priority as we went into town and bought an engagement ring with diamonds in it. You couldn't see them but there was rationing and everything was short, so it was right for the times. That's my story anyway. We agreed to write to each other and there were tears on parting, as I had no idea how long I would be abroad.

At the end of my leave I had to report to Warrington where we were told that we would be sailing on the S. S. Empress of Scotland in two days time, but were not told where to. We were loaded into trucks and driven to the quayside in Liverpool, where a large passenger liner was berthed. She was a passenger liner that had been converted to a troop ship.

There were only about thirty R.A.F. guys, all aircrew who had been grounded, varying from Sergeants to Warrant Officers and all ex-operational aircrew. We were led up the gang-plank and walked around the deck to an area near the bow which had been covered over to form a sort of accommodation with bunk beds.

There were no lockers so we had to stow our kit bags against the wall and throughout the trip we had to forage for kit. Initially we were very unhappy, as we did not think this was fit accommodation for 'we heroes.' But when we went for a meal, we were enlightened.

Several hundred Army men had been marched on and were taken below. When we went down to the dining room several decks down, we encountered a large number of very angry soldiers. They were in the bottom deck in accommodation not fit for animals, and were charging back up on deck.

We followed to watch, and an Army Warrant Officer lined them up on the top deck, said that he agreed the conditions were appalling, and that he would lead them off the ship. Unfortunately, the crew had removed the gang planks so there was a long delay.

Then the W/O reappeared and ordered the first platoon up to the bow where he had found escape nets rolled up and fixed to the hand rails. They cut the restraining ropes and the nets unrolled down the side of the ship on to the dockside. The W/O ordered the men to follow him in orderly fashion—no dashing off.

'You will form up on the quay in a proper manner and await my orders.' he said.

So all the soldiers climbed down the ropes and formed up in three ranks on the quay just as if they were on parade. The W/O marched them off and they disappeared towards the town. We, being nosey, went down to have a look. We thoroughly agreed with them, but an R.A.F. officer suddenly appeared and ordered us out of there quickly.

'The R.A.F. does not want to be mixed up in this,' he said, 'We will stay aboard tonight and see what tomorrow brings.' We went for our evening meal and were very surprised at the fine quality of the food served by the Merchant Navy crew.

The next morning we went to the showers and dressed ready for breakfast. We all started complaining about our hair, which was as stiff as a board. The Navy crew all started laughing and said that the soap in the shower was salt-water soap and you did not use it on hair. So we all had to rewash our hair in the wash hand basins.

Just after lunch, the Flight Lieutenant appeared and said that we were all to go on a three-day pass while the army sorted their troops out, and report back to the ship, on the assumption that we were going.

Much to Margaret's delight, instead of being on the high seas, I was calling in at Stephenson Clarke at Cardiff docks where she worked as a short hand typist. There was much humour amongst the other girls but she was allowed to leave straightaway with me.

Our unexpected two days together was great, but off I had to go again. When we all assembled at the ship we were told to get on board as the Army had agreed to put the soldiers on another deck, and they were all on the ship and ready to sail. Their new deck was a bit better than the previous one, but it was stifling and crowded, so we went back to our main deck level much more content. The ship sailed as it was getting dark, so there was not a lot to see and we all took to our beds early.

In the middle of the night there was uproar. A storm was a blowing and the ship was rolling and bucking in violent seas. It seemed that the entire body of passengers was on deck being sick and moaning. Fortunately, I and Matt, another flight engineer, were not seasick, and although unable to sleep, were not in any discomfort. Come morning the decks were lined with moaning, green-looking men, both R.A.F. and Army.

Matt and I went down to breakfast. The dining room was almost deserted and we enjoyed a large breakfast of bacon and eggs. When we had finished we both made a large egg and bacon sandwich and took it up on deck offering the 'sickly types' breakfast. It was not well received, and we were unpopular for some time afterwards!

The journey through the Bay of Biscay was rough all the way and it wasn't until we turned into the Mediterranean Sea that things became calm and sunny. We then enjoyed a beautiful trip to Port Said at the beginning of the Suez Canal.

The ship pulled into a berth and was besieged by 'bum boats,' native rowing boats loaded with fruit and goods, which they tried to sell us by throwing up lines with pouches attached. However, they had few takers, and they became quite abusive, and the language was an education, even for service men.

We stayed overnight and the next day sailed through the canal into the Red Sea. In some areas the ship was very close to the bank and although it was desolate country there were often natives on the bank making rude gestures and lifting up their robes.

We did not stop at Port Suez and sailed into the Indian Ocean in brilliant sunshine, being entertained by the porpoises jumping into the air and swimming right by the bow of the ship, diving in and out of the bow wave. Once out into the ocean there was nothing to see but sea, it quickly became boring and there was very little to do.

An Army officer set up quiz competitions with Army vs. R.A.F., and then organized a concert party where rehearsals were open to all. We sat in the big hall and watched the antics and enjoyed the mistakes, which were funnier than the correct version. Eventually the show was put on and it was surprisingly good, with a great deal of talent exhibited.

On the way to Burma, May, 1946.

We had been at sea nearly two weeks when we were assembled in the hall and told our destination was Singapore. We did not stop anywhere prior to reaching our destination. We disembarked before the Army, were loaded into trucks and taken to Tengah, an ex-Prisoner of War camp, where the accommodation was dreadful. It was merely a transit camp and we were told we would be shipped out in a day or two. In fact we were there a week. Singapore was not in a very good state. As well as the battle damage, the Japanese had destroyed much of the City, and Changi jail was a nightmare.

We left on time but were appalled at the sight of a native troop ship awaiting us at the docks. We were told to get on board and despite our protests, had to do so. Fortunately for us, the native troops were pushed down below. We did not even look at their accommodation, as we were not pleased with ours.

We were the same thirty airmen who had been on the Empress of Scotland, and were supposed to go down one deck. The weather fortunately was dry and very warm, so we all stayed on deck and slept there. The food was dreadful too, so we were in for a rotten journey. We had not sailed long before we were told we were bound for Rangoon, and it could not come quickly enough. However, it took a week of great discomfort to reach Rangoon

After docking we were hustled into lorries and taken through the city of which we saw little and were soon heading North through tropical countryside and rice fields. Some twenty miles north of Rangoon we came to a large aerodrome, with a large gate and neat garden edges and white stones set in the earth that said, 'Welcome to Mingaladon.'

We were driven to a large hutted encampment near the main buildings of the airfield. Each hut was framed of thick bamboo with matting forming walls to a three foot height. Above that was open to a thatched roof of palm fronds. These huts were known as 'bashas.' The single beds were the usual metal framed type, but each had a mosquito net draped at the top end. We were separated out into about eight per hut, which was quite roomy, with decent locker facilities and a couple of trestle tables in the centre.

We were greeted by a Flight Lieutenant who said, 'I don't know what you are here for, but this is your billet and the Sergeants' mess is at the bottom of this row of huts.'

He gave us a leaflet with meal times and general information on the camp, and said that we would have further information tomorrow. He said that the most important points were not to go out to the toilet at night, and before putting boots or shoes on in the morning, turn them out as snakes loved the warmth.

We asked where the washroom and toilet was and he pointed to a low basha type building about 20 yards away on top of a bank of earth. The hut was 15 yards long and inside was a long seat on a box almost the length of the building with a series of large holes in the top. 'That's it,' he said.

We learned that grass snakes about 10 feet long and very thick, liked to sleep on the top of the box, and seemed to be there every night. Needless to say we didn't use the toilet at night. We took a long time to accept that they were harmless.

We unpacked our kit and went down to the mess where we found that we had a separate dining room, also a basha, and all the staff were Indians. The meals were called by their Indian names and it was difficult at first to recognise them. However, the mess was very pleasant and we were allowed two bottles of beer a day. Otherwise, we could drink spirits which were very plentiful and dirt cheap. Spirits were not my scene, however. Cigarettes were plentiful and cheap and were packed in round tins of fifty.

The next day we were addressed by a Wingco who said that the prime function of the drome was mail collection and delivery. Twice weekly a Dakota left with the mail for Ceylon and brought back the mail for us and Singapore, which was dropped off on the way back and where they collected their mail for the next trip to Ceylon. He said that some of us could volunteer to be baggage handlers, but there would not be much flying as there were so many who wanted to fly.

For those not wishing to do this, there were only general duties and there would be a lot of spare time. He said that as there were quite a lot of Japanese P.O.W.'s in the camp, all the mucky jobs were done by them. We were cautioned not to get involved with them and they were to be left to the Army chaps, who were in charge of them. If we wanted something done, we asked the Army.

I volunteered immediately for the baggage handling and was told to report the next morning to the mail shed. Actually it was a hangar but no one called it anything but the mail shed. The next day I duly turned up and was told to help load the mail sacks into the Dakota, which was outside on the tarmac. I was surprised at the quantity until it was explained that this was almost the entire mail for the whole of the Army and R.A.F. in the Far East, as it was all collected and delivered to either Singapore or Mingaladon.

I enquired about the trip to Ceylon but was told to get in the queue. Apparently I was going to have to put my name on the list and I would probably get one or two flights a month. I immediately went into the mail office and put my name down, so I was at least in the front of our lot.

Work in this area was only two days a week usually for the 'extras' so the rest of the time was spent idling the time away playing cards or football or just reading. Letters came regularly from Marg and I had to respond, although it was not always easy to find a lot to write about. I made do with lots of slush!

In one letter Marg told me how a friend had told her that the jewelers in Queen Street, Cardiff had some gold wedding rings so she had dashed down there and stood in a queue and was successful in getting one. She was the proud owner of a wedding ring and I guess that meant it was all up for me, my chasing of girls was over.

I made enquiries and found there was no rugby so went to join the soccer team. It turned out that they needed a goalkeeper.

'Well that's a bit of luck for me, that's my position', I lied. Fortunately the standard was not very high and I made out O.K. and joined the team.

I also spent quite a bit of time in the mess playing solo whist and although we played for money, not a lot changed hands. After a couple of days I noticed a W/O Navigator standing watching but he never played. One day after we finished a session he approached me and said, 'You play a decent game of cards, do you play bridge?' I told him I had never played bridge and he said that I was just the chap he was looking for.

In Civvy Street he was a professional bridge player and he was looking for someone who had never played bridge to teach his system. He explained that there were a few systems for playing and he had developed his own, but he needed someone with no preconceptions.

He said that there was an army camp down the road from the drome and that there were some very good players who organised games on a regular basis and the stakes were quite high. He said we could make a profit if I learnt the game and played with him.

I said I was not fussy if the stakes were high, as I did not have any money to throw away. He persuaded me to learn the game and give it a go. For a couple of weeks we were in the mess almost every day I had off. He taught me how to play bridge, then his method, which was based on the Blackwood system but amended to his ideas. We became quite good friends and, as he did not drink much, it was a good way to pass a lot of time.

Finally, he said I was ready to go to a game at the army camp and arranged for us to go one evening. I was nervous at first but suddenly realised that in almost every hand I was the dummy and so I watched carefully and saw that he was leading the bidding so that he played the hand.

When the evening finished we were just in pocket so I felt relieved. He said that we would have another couple of sessions to improve my playing before coming again. He said that my bidding was fine but I needed more practice in the playing of the hands.

The next time we went I played a great deal better and we did reasonably well. We played a lot of bridge after that, and although I did not make a lot of money, at least it did not cost me any.

It finally became my turn to fly and I reported early at the mail shed. We loaded the Dakota and then I was told to get in and sort myself out somewhere to sit. I sat with four other 'ex-op' types on the mailbags and fortunately could see out of a window. We took off and flew out to sea over Rangoon with the Golden Pagoda standing out reflecting the bright sunshine. First of all there was just sea, but then there was the coastline and we could see the island and landed at Singapore.

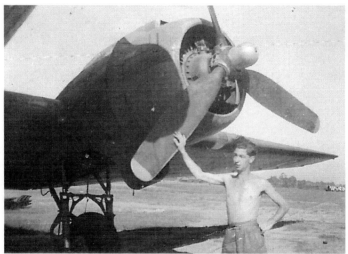

On the mail run, Burma, 1946.

Their incoming bags were unloaded and we loaded the outgoing ones. We went off to the mess and had lunch and were soon airborne again. It was quite a long flight to Ceylon with nothing to look at except the ocean and we were dozing most of the way until we landed. We unloaded all the mail and went to the mess, where after a wash and brush up we had a meal.

A corporal with whom I had struck up an acquaintance during my working in the mail shed suggested we go into Colombo and look around, and I agreed. We jumped into a lorry going into town and were taken into the city. It was quite an experience because it was the first eastern city I had been in that wasn't a mess due to the war.

However, apart from the main streets where there were some nice shops, it was dirty and the natives were very belligerent if we did not buy from their stalls or shops. They were really more like holes in the wall than shops. Still, it was an experience, and I enjoyed the visit. We caught the lorry back to the drome and were billeted in a reasonable barrack block building for the night. Next morning we loaded up the mail and off we went back to Rangoon and Mingaladon.

I only did one more flight in the rest of my stay, and even the loading stopped as they started using the Japanese to do the loading. So life became a boring routine relieved only by the mad antics of the types who had been out there a long time.

There were lots of scorpions around the unpaved areas and most of us avoided them like the plague. These guys however would catch one and bring it into the mess where they would ring it with petrol and set light to the fumes. The scorpion would run around the circle until it reached the exact point at which it had started and would then sting itself in the neck, committing suicide. Sometimes they would bring one in suspended on string by the tail and hang it on the dartboard. They would then try to kill it with darts. The first time was interesting but the second was just mad.

They also used to go snake hunting and were always delighted if they captured a 'crate.' These were a beautiful silver color with a thin blood red line down their belly. The trouble was, if you were bitten by a crate, they were deadly poisonous, so this we avoided totally.

The soccer team entered the local Army Stations Cup. There were six Army teams, so they invited two R.A.F. teams to make up the number. It was a knock-out cup played on a home and away basis. The final would only be one game.

We won the first game easily and were one game all in the second, which we won by one goal scored in the last minute. The matches drew a lot of attention and when we went to the Army sites we were very well entertained, and so we had to do likewise when we entertained them. They really were great afternoons and evenings.

We were now in the final and it was decided that the game would be played in the adjacent Army camp, which was a neutral ground and convenient for both teams. We had a chap who had played semi-professional for some small town team and was a good player and who became our coach. He gave me lots of useful tips particularly about corners and penalties, which I listened to intently, since I really had no experience at all playing soccer.

The day came and half of the R.A.F. personnel came to the field where we also found almost as many Army types. There was a lot of bantering but it was all good-natured. The first half ended one all and not long into the second our full back brought an Army guy down in the penalty area and my main fear was realised.

Then I remembered what I had been told, 'Amateurs will always look where they are going to kick the ball.' It worked and I managed to push the ball away for a corner, which delighted everyone on our team. Unfortunately, they scored later on in that half and we lost the game. Still, we were royally entertained and had a great evening with free beer for both teams.

We had been in Mingaladon for two months, and it seemed that we were waiting forever for our demob (demobilisation). Finally, we were told that our papers had arrived and that the process would start the next day. We had no idea what 'the process' meant but the on the morrow we were given appointment times, staggered so that the 30 or so of us who had papers did the rounds.

We had a medical, then a Mensa type test and then had an interview with the Education Officer. He told us the results of the tests; I was healthy, intelligent and had a Mensa score of 150. He said that I should try to go to university and that my R.A.F. records would be sufficient to satisfy the entrance requirement.

He said I should aim to be an architect or accountant, or anything at that sort of professional level.

At that time I just wanted to get on a boat and go home as Marg had told me that everything was organized for the wedding. I didn't reckon I had much time for anything else. More importantly, I had no job or prospects, and no money.

About a week later we were taken down to Rangoon docks where we boarded another converted cruise ship, and once again we were lucky to be accommodated in a deck near the main deck. We were only about thirty Air Force types against many hundreds of Army, and as we were all aircrew, we were treated very well.

The journey home was great as there were lots of organized activities and many inter-service competitions. The weather was good and we had a very nice, long, relaxing trip. We docked in Liverpool and were immediately transported to Warrington.

It only took a few days to sort us out and we were at the demob centre, collecting civilian clothing. We went into a large store and it was just like being kitted out with uniform so long ago. The guys behind the counter just said, 'Size,' and threw it at us until we got to the suits. There it was 'Grey, navy or brown?' and 'Small, medium or large?' and they slid one across the counter. Then they gave us a ration book, a pay book and pay chits for six weeks demob leave, together with a railway warrant to get home.

They took all our uniforms and R.A.F. stuff, so we had nothing in the way of mementoes. I did manage to keep my flying log-book, however, so at least I had a record of my flying career and operational trips.

Next Page

My Royal Air Force Certificate of Service and Release Papers. The recommendation reads 'A hard worker who uses his intelligence at all times. He hopes to become a draughtsman & also to take an engineering degree. I consider that he would make full use of any assistance which could be offered to him (including a full time university education). He has a good personality and an excellent character.' It is dated 14 April, 1947.

My Royal Air Force Certificate of Service and Release Papers.

Chapter 14

BACK TO CIVILIAN LIFE

The train journey home seemed endless but finally the train drew into Cardiff station and there was Margaret, looking gorgeous and I was enveloped in a huge hug. I can't say that I was as smart as she. We went to Penarth Road where my mother and father were waiting, and before long the conversation turned to the imminent wedding.

Marg told me the arrangements: We were to be married in St. James Church in Newport Road, and the reception was to be in her mother and dad's house in Treharris Street.

Marg had a white dress and veil. I don't know how since clothing was rationed, but she did! Her cousin, Beryl was to be bridesmaid and she had a lovely dress too. My only duty was to announce that Bob the bomb aimer, would be my best man, and was coming down from Lancashire on his motor bike. He arrived the day before the wedding and took a present of a wall clock off the pillion of his bike, unfortunately in pieces. Still he replaced it later so all was well.

My R.A.F. career was from 23rd January, 1944 to 31st May, 1947. From a naïve, very young lad, I survived to become a happily married man, a father of four very successful children, and nine grandchildren. Margaret and I have now been happily married for 63 years, and her help in obtaining the accurate records for my story and her patience as editor, are very much appreciated.

When I left the R.A.F., I was 21 years old.

Margaret and I are married, June 14, 1947.

CHAPTER 16.

AUSTRALIAN VISIT

On Christmas Day, 2001, the telephone rang and it was Alf ringing to wish us a Happy Christmas. During the long conversation he said we should visit him in Australia. Yes, we said thinking, Oh Aye, just like that. However later that day Roger (our son living in the U.S.A.) rang and during our conversation asked, 'Why not?'

Some few weeks later we sorted around and finally booked with Emirates Airline and flew to Sidney. Alf and his daughter Ros, met us at the Airport and took us to Manly, where we stayed that night in a hotel. The following day we drove to Cowra, a journey of about seven hours.

Alf and his wife Alma live on a farm just outside the town and he had said it was by a river and trees. We drove out of Cowra about a mile along a country road, turned into a field and drove right across it. Suddenly, there in isolation was a farmhouse with large water tanks behind. I said to Alf, 'Where's the river and trees?'

'Look there,' he said, and way in the distance were trees and apparently, a river. We stayed for a week before going into Sydney.

On the Wednesday Alma took us out as Alf, who was the local Estate Agent, had to go to work. We went to an artificial beach created on a lake and on the way back stopped at a trout farm where we bought some fish for dinner. I suggested to Alma that I would cook dinner much, I would say, to Alf's disgust.

However, I did cook and we had a very nice meal with quite a large volume of wine. After dinner Alf disappeared and came back with his Air Force uniform jacket on, not meeting at the front, and his officer's cap perched on the top of his head. It was a sight to behold. Needless to say, the stories then unfolded and we learned a great deal about Alf Cowley.

Alf in his uniform and flight gear and me in Cowra, Australia, 2001, after a few glasses of wine!

Alf was born in 1921 and at 17 joined the militia corps, saying he was 18. He was called up upon the outbreak of war. On 8th May, 1940 he claimed he was 21, and eligible for overseas service with the Australian Imperial Forces.

At that time, he transferred to the ATF and joined the Second Anti-Tank Regiment as a Gun Sergeant. The unit served in Palestine, North Africa and Syria, where he was Mentioned in Dispatches. The unit returned to Australia in 1942 in anticipation of a possible invasion by Japan.

Alf and me in Cowra, Australia, 2001.

Late in 1942 Alf re-mustered to the Royal Australian Air Force and trained as a pilot in Australia and Canada. He proved to be an exceptional pilot, and was commissioned on passing out. Alf arrived in the U.K. in late 1943.

During that stay he took me aside and said, 'You know Ron, you were a far better Flight Engineer than you gave yourself credit for.'

He then reminded me that he had demonstrated his intolerance of anyone not carrying out his job properly by dismissing the mid-upper gunner who did not measure up.

More than that, he said, 'At Bottesford you topped not only the Flight Engineer's course, but if you remember, you did my examination and topped the Pilot's course as well!'

'You have every right to be very proud of your service career,' Alf said.

I guess I am.